The Reality of Hell and the Goodness of God

The Reality of Hell and the Goodness of God

HAROLD T. BRYSON

LIVING STUDIES
Tyndale House Publishers, Inc.
Wheaton, Illinois

First printing, May 1984
Library of Congress Catalog Card Number 83-51674
ISBN 0-8423-5279-1
Copyright © 1984 by Harold T. Bryson
Printed in the United States of America

To JUDITH, *my wife,*
who shares earth's greatest relationship

To WILLIAM *and* THOMAS, *my sons,*
who bring earth's greatest responsibility

CONTENTS

PREFACE

Bible subjects are never out of date. Inspired ideas rise to prominence according to people's needs and interests. Extreme social inhumanities cause us to look again at the social implications of the gospel. Recurring outbreaks of sin and evil inspire studies on Satan, demons, and the occult.

Personal problems such as fear, guilt, loneliness, boredom, depression, and anxiety move writers to look at the scriptural views of human needs. The movement of God in the lives of people incites in-depth studies on the Holy Spirit. Broken marriages and friendships arouse interest in what the Bible says about interpersonal relationships. Depressing world conditions incite interest in the final end of history.

Christianity may be the "old time religion," but it is neither obsolete nor out of date. People of every generation want to know about life after death. Since death looms on the horizon for all of us, many want to know about the life beyond. Many people today have become interested in *eschatology*, the study of last things. Some say that we should not talk about the life beyond, believing that it leads to morbid preoccupation with the next world. Henry David Thoreau said, "I'm not interested in questions on immortality. One world at a time—that's my motto. Do the duty that lies close at hand here and don't worry about the hereafter." Some talk about the life beyond in terms of *reincarnation*, the belief that the souls of the dead will later return to earth in new forms. Books which discuss reincarnation appear in many modern bookstores today. Some contend that no life exists beyond the grave and some of these say that belief in a future life exists only in man's subconscious as a wish fulfillment.

Others believe in *spiritism,* trying through seances to communicate with people beyond the grave.

Christians, however, since New Testament times, have interpreted the Bible to teach that we will live forever, either in heaven or in hell. Add these discussions to numerous other ideas, and you can readily agree that talk on life after death is not obsolete. Very few will agree with Paschal's statement, "Since men have not succeeded in curing death, they have decided . . . not to think about it at all." People of all cultures have queries and assertions about life beyond the grave.

Very little has been written, and few people today are talking about hell. The idea might prevail that the concept of hell belongs to the antiquities of a former generation. Because the subject doesn't come up in discussions, sermons, and books, one might think hell has been eliminated. The frivolous use of the word in profanity and joking might have presented the image that there is no hell.

But every now and then the subject comes up for discussion. People often ask, "Does the Bible teach the reality of hell?" "What kind of place is hell?"

Our generation deserves a realistic, biblical concept of the final state of the unsaved. They have been furnished other biblical studies for various interests, so they deserve also a scriptural approach to the subject of hell.

This study owes its origin to the keen interest of hundreds of university students in a retreat setting. The leaders and students requested that I lead a study of the Book of Revelation. They wanted to hear lectures on the last book in the Bible, a book which contains strange visions and unusual creatures. When I came to Revelation 20, I thought the students would ask whether Christ would come before or after the millennium or whether or not there would actually be a millennium. Instead, they did not ask me one question about the expression "a thousand years." It was phrases such as "bottomless pit," "lake of fire and brimstone," "tormented day and night forever," and "second death" that triggered their interest.

One student asked, "Preacher, do you really believe in hell?" I replied, "Yes, I do."

My affirmation spurred other questions: "Why do you believe in hell?" "If hell is real, why do we not hear more about it?" "What is a good book on hell?" "How could a good God permit such a bad place as hell to exist?" "Do you believe that people suffer forever?" "What kind of place is hell?" "Is the fire real?" "How can there be darkness and fire at the same time?" "Will all people there suffer the same?"

I was amazed at their intense interest, and was deeply embarrassed that I couldn't give them satisfactory answers. My studies on the biblical teaching about hell had been limited throughout my life.

Prodded by these students, I thought, read, and restudied the Scriptures. I carefully looked at all the verses about the experiences of the unsaved. After looking at a number of theology books and commentaries, I discovered that very little had been written on hell. As I read and talked with people about the subject, I felt that many other people had serious questions also. They desired to know what the Bible said about it. They were not satisfied with the frivolity or with the silence.

Hell is real, according to the Bible. It deserves serious consideration. One should neither laugh at the idea of hell, nor should it be explained away. The reasoning of one student is understandable. She said, "If hell is taught in the Bible, let us assert its reality and describe its nature. Or, if hell is not taught in the Bible, let us dispel the rumor." Any serious student knows how often the Bible talks about hell, so the topic needs to be explored.

The purpose of this book is to express my thoughts on hell and to ask you to think with me. Without apology I say, "Yes, there is a hell." The Bible teaches that there is a fundamental difference between the fate of the saved and the unsaved. There will be a final separation of the redeemed from the unredeemed. The unsaved experience the horrifying reality of hell. Being perfectly honest, I sought several times in my studies to eliminate the idea of a literal hell from my theology. I sought to substitute it with universalism and then with annihilationism. But the New Testament gave me no escape.

The biblical doctrine of hell goes far deeper than grotesque ideas of flames, brimstone, and pitchforks. It teaches that hell is a life of separation from God on earth which leads to final separation after death. In this life the unsaved experience estrangement and existential despair. The life of the unsaved on earth is a preview of hell, but it is not all there is of it. No discussion of hell should be restricted either to now or to the future. Hell is not just a bad place in the future. It is also the frustrating experiences outside of Christ now. It is the extreme state of life apart from God. If a person lives without opening his life to God, he or she will be separated forever from God's presence.

What is the best way to write a book on hell? Perhaps it would help to be biblical, honest, and gentle. One should strive to avoid being dogmatic, too imaginative, and free of exaggeration. Books which interest me get me involved in the thought process. The reader wants to be involved with the author. Whether we listen to a sermon or read a book, we want to be involved. Using this criterion, I decided to write a "think along" book on hell.

This work is not a theology book for you to memorize in class. These chapters are not sermons for you to read. The book is no pontifical edict intended to teach the view that every Christian holds about hell. Naturally, you may disagree at times. These responses are natural elements of thinking along. During the process, I hope you get involved. Along the way you will ask questions and seek more information.

I am deeply indebted to numerous people for the way I think. Pastors furnished me early beginnings in biblical theology. College and seminary professors motivated me to think further, deeper, and longer. During the process of thinking and writing about hell, two congregations listened, questioned, and encouraged me, and allowed time for thinking and for writing. These churches tolerated several absences, allowing me to share my thinking with college and church groups. The First Baptist Church of Carthage, Mississippi, and the Eastdale Baptist Church of Montgomery, Alabama, deserve commendation.

Two church secretaries rendered tremendous service amid other secretarial duties. Mrs. Marguerite Givan from the Carthage church typed the original drafts. Mrs. Kelly Lawson of the Eastdale church typed the final copy. Mrs. Ruth Ann Kinchen rendered a valuable service in typing the revised edition for Tyndale House Publishers. Many interested persons read the manuscript and offered insight on how my thoughts could be stated more forcefully and clearly.

Finally, but not of small importance, I am grateful to my wife, Judith. She has been a sustaining, motivating influence in this project. She probed and helped me to think. Unquestionably, she is my favorite "thinker along." She shares at every phase of my ministry. This book has been no exception. Amid the responsibilities for two energy-packed boys, she took time to read and to help me in the effort.

ONE
YES, THERE IS A HELL!

Belief in the reality of hell arises out of any serious study of the Bible. In recent years there has been an increased interest in the study of Scripture. Many people are searching to discover truth both for the sake of knowledge and for the sake of the Bible's ability to be a guide for living. Students are seeking to know what the Scriptures meant when they were first written, and what these passages mean in today's world.

The study of some Bible passages sometimes brings confusion. There often seem to be contradictions of new insights with traditional teachings. Or, there could be a discrepancy between what people say the Bible means and what the biblical writers intended to say.

This difference between what people say and what the Bible teaches is noticed especially on the subject of hell. Therefore, more study of the Bible is needed to know just what the Bible teaches about hell.

Many questions arise about whether hell is a real place or not. The silence on the subject of hell in today's world causes some people to wonder if what the Bible teaches about hell is true. Not many books have been written about this serious subject, and few sermons are preached about it. The silence on one hand and the teaching about hell in the Scriptures on the other hand do not seem to coincide.

The profane jesting also causes some to question whether or not there is a hell. The word *hell* is a part of the vocabulary of many people, but only as an idle curse word. On many occasions, the cheering sections at sporting events tell their opponents to "go to hell." These all make hell seem unreal. Subconsciously the profanity and jesting cause people to think less seriously about this most serious place.

In addition to the strange silence and the jesting, the imaginative descriptions given of hell seem to lessen people's belief in its reality. At times some preachers have depicted hell more with grotesque physical descriptions than with what the Bible says about it. They depict hell as a huge inferno, and show God as a harsh judge who takes pleasure in the destruction of the wicked. These descriptions often miss the truth about hell as taught by the Bible. It is easy to see why people want to know what the Bible really teaches.

Many people today doubt or deny that hell is real. Some claim to have outgrown what they heard in the church as a child. Others say that hell is nothing more than a symbol of man's evil ways. Still others regard hell as a myth, while some try to make the Bible say that everyone will be saved eventually. Then there are those who say the Bible teaches that one day the wicked will be annihilated. In Marc Connelly's classic play, Green Pastures, the angel Gabriel reported to the Lord about conditions immediately following Noah's flood. The angel said, "Lawd, de're ain't nothin' nailed down any more. Ever'thin' nailed down is comin' loose." Many biblical truths which had been affirmed for years seem now to be "coming loose."

But there is a hell which the Bible teaches, not like the place that some people describe. Some descriptions are nothing more than sadistic imaginations. The hell the Bible describes as the place of future punishment of the wicked cannot be laughed at or explained away. It needs to be thought about with a Bible in hand, a thinking mind, and a prayer to know the truth.

DENIALS

What makes people read about hell in the Bible and yet deny that there is a real hell? Strangely enough, most of those who don't believe in hell know a little about Scripture. The atheists and agnostics are not the main opponents of hell. Some people who read and study the Bible are the ones who build cases against it. Origen, the famous biblical interpreter of the second century, denied that hell exists forever, saying that the punishments of the condemned are not endless but remedial. He said that the devil himself was capable of amelioration. This man had a profound influence on how others interpreted the Bible. He rejected the allegorical interpretation which prevailed in his day and insisted on a historical-grammatical approach to Scripture. But his interpretations caused many to adhere to his idea on hell. Such notable men as Basil, Clement, Gregory of Nyssa, and Gregory of Nazianzus believed what Origen taught about hell.

Many Bible scholars of the nineteenth and twentieth centuries deny the existence of hell. Friedrich Schleiermacher, an influential German theologian, wrote in several of his books that the future will involve a general restoration of all human souls. Horace Bushness and Lyman Abbott taught that the wicked would in the end waste away and be completely destroyed. Though not a formal theologian, Alfred Lord Tennyson in his poem "In Memoriam," helped to weaken the belief in eternal punishment more than the writings of many biblical scholars. Frederic William Farrar (1831-1903), dean of Canterbury, taught that most people would eventually be saved. He wrote about the possibility of repentance beyond the grave.

Turning to the twentieth century we find many Bible students who deny the reality of eternal punishment. Many of today's writers think that hell refers just to a person's hard experiences in this life, as heard in the expression of someone who is "going through hell." Existential writers such as Jean Paul Sartre cause people to think of hell as nothing more than meaningless despair of life on earth. Leslie Weatherhead, pastor of City Temple in London for many years, denied the doctrine of eternal punishment. He said that "God will eventually bring everyone into the kingdom of God."[1] To be honest, the writings of such Bible scholars as Karl Barth and Emil Brunner are hard to grasp by most lay persons. Karl Barth believed that all men are elected and redeemed in Jesus Christ and need only to be told about this. Emil Brunner strongly rejected Barth's universalism, but he argued for a second chance beyond the grave. Paul Tillich taught that Christianity lessened the dread of death by three attempts: reincarnation, bodiless existency, and purgatory. Nikolai Berdyaev, the Russian existentialist, wrote about hell: "A higher and maturer consciousness cannot accept the old-fashioned idea of hell; but a light-hearted sentimental optimistic rejection of it is equally untenable. Hell unquestionably exists ... but it ... is temporal."[2] To be sure, one has a hard time finding a strong belief in a real hell from statements such as these.

Many religious groups such as Jehovah's Witnesses, Christian Science, Unitarian-Universalists, and Mormonism cause people to doubt the reality of hell. One common trait of these religious groups is their denial of eternal punishment. Christian Science teaches that hell involves "mortal belief; error; lust; remorse; hatred; revenge; sin, sickness, death, suffering, and self-imposed agony, effects of sin, that which worketh abomination or maketh a lie."[3] This group contends that when a person dies he moves to another level of conscious existence where he will have other chances to correct errors.

Charles Taze Russell was born in 1852 in Pittsburgh. His parents were Presbyterian, but he joined the Congregationalists because he thought they were more liberal. At the age of seventeen, he gave up the church, primarily because of their teachings on hell. Russell denied hell and taught that the wicked would be completely annhilated. Russell's followers, known as Jehovah's Witnesses, loudly opposed the idea of hell on the basis that a God who tortured his creatures would not be a God of love.

Mormons believe in hell but not as an endless existence. Mormons or Latter-Day Saints deny the doctrine of one heaven and one hell. They teach that life after death involves three levels: celestial, terrestrial, and telestial. The celestial level includes Mormons in an intermediate state who will eventually become gods. The terrestrial level includes Christians and other persons who rejected the Mormon message. The telestial level is reserved for those currently in hell who await a final resurrection. Mormons teach that these will in the end be saved and not be punished forever.

There could be some reasons why people deny hell. Some deny hell because of their temperament. Their gentle and kind nature will not allow them to believe in such terrible ideas as eternal hell. They are like the sentimental parents who do not notice the mistakes of their children. They often refuse to accept either the truth or the results of their children's sin. These people would, of course, have trouble accepting that sin has to be punished. As a result, they think of God as a submissive and permissive being.

Others deny that hell is real on the basis of theology. Using various moral arguments some seek to explain away any mention of hell in the Bible. It is said that hell contradicts the idea of God's goodness. Frederic W. Farrar said that the doctrine of endless punishment made many people into infidels. Using rationalistic arguments, many people ask, "Do you think a good God could torment sinners forever?" This line of reasoning touches us, and convinces many that hell must not exist.

Theologians often contend that the eternal presence of hell seems to defeat the sovereignty of God. They reason that if hell exists forever, then God seems to have "lost the war" against evil. Therefore, people who reason this way affirm that the Lord must have the final victory over evil. They conclude that God in the end defeats evil either by everyone being saved or by all the wicked being destroyed, making it seem that there's no need for hell.

Other people deny that hell exists on the basis of modern science. Some assume that discoveries of science in the twentieth century render belief in future life impossible. Using science to show that the chemical parts of the body are dissolved after death, they deny that a body could be resurrected. Also, the theory of organic evolution tries to show man's common origin with lower life forms. Evolution destroys the basis for believing that man has a higher destiny than any other creature. Some naively insist that our putting man and machines in space leaves no place for what the Bible teaches about heaven and hell. It has been assumed that if man finds no evidence of heaven in space then there is likewise no hell located in the other direction. This whole logic fails to consider that the Bible's use of up and down did not speak about space but of spiritual realities.

Others seek to disprove hell by saying that there cannot be fire and darkness at the same time. They contend that there cannot be a fire which does not consume. These people do not understand the spiritual message conveyed by the metaphors of fire or darkness. Psychologists looking into the workings of man's mind contend that man's thought about life beyond the grave is created by a subconscious wish-fulfillment. Perhaps we should hasten to observe that no fact yet discovered by biology, anthropology, astrology, or psychology disproves what the Bible teaches about a future life. So the idea of a life beyond the grave is as possible as ever.

Many people reject the unreal pictures which are presented about hell, so their denials are not so much a rejection of hell as the disdain of some humanistic ideas about hell. Exaggerated descriptions have been presented which cause many people to deny hell from a humanitarian point of view. John Milton described hell as follows:

At once as far as angels ken he views
the dismal situation waste and wild:
A dungeon horrible, on all sides round
As one great furnace flamed, yet from these flames.
From those flames
No light, but rather darkness visible
Several only to discover sight of woe,
Regions of sorrow, doleful shades,
Where peace and rest can never dwell, hope never comes
That comes to all; but torture without end
Still rages, and a fiery deluge, fed
With ever-burning sulphur unconsumed.[4]

It is difficult to identify with many dreadful descriptions of hell. Michelangelo in *The Last Judgement* painted God on a high throne separating the souls of men, sending some to bliss and others to torment. Dante Alighieri (better known as Dante) in his poem *The Divine Comedy* described dramatically the awful physical torment of hell. Many a person has formed his concept of hell from Doré's imaginative drawings illustrating Dante's *The Divine Comedy*. Venerable Bede, a Middle Age churchman, described a person in hell with the flames of fire gushing out from his ears and eyes and nostrils and at every pore. Another medieval theologian described the tortures of hell: "The blood was boiling in her veins, the brains were boiling in her skull, and marrow in her bones." These pictures of torment cause many people to dismiss the idea of hell from their minds. Rather than seeking to discover what Christ taught about future punishment, they listen to others, who speak, not about the hell taught in Scripture, but the hell conceived and presented by the human mind.

No reasons seem to be enough to deny that hell is real. Perhaps most people just wish that it wasn't.

DECLARATIONS

What prompts a person to believe in hell? The answer is simple—the clear teachings of God's Word. Read the Bible from beginning to end. You will learn that God responded very quickly in judgment against sin. As you read further in the Old Testament, you see that sin brings terrible consequences. By the time you read through the New Testament it becomes clear that good and evil will be separated by God's judgment. Many metaphors and images from the New Testament describe eternal punishment. If you notice carefully, most of the teaching about hell comes from Jesus. One seems to have at least three options about the Bible's teaching of hell. First, you can refuse everything the Bible teaches. But this would open Pandora's Box for rejecting other cardinal doctrines. If you deny what the Bible teaches about hell, what stops you from denying other New Testament teachings such as the incarnation or the resurrection of Christ? Second, you can ignore only what the Bible says about hell. Perhaps many people take this option. They read verses on hell but choose to ignore them. Then, the last and most reasonable option is to read, study, and accept the biblical reality of hell.

Now look at what the Bible says about the word *hell*. The English word *hell* comes from the Old English word *helan*, meaning "to hide or cover." The word *hell* appears fifty-two times in the King James Version of the Bible. It has been translated from one Hebrew word, *sheol*, and three Greek words: *gehenna*, *hades*, and *tartarus*. The Hebrew word *sheol* literally refers to a deep pit under the earth. As a figure it refers to the shadowy realm of the dead. Usually when *sheol* is translated "hell" in the King James Version of the Old Testament it does not refer to eternal punishment, but to the place where good and evil people continue to exist after death. More recent translations of Scripture render the word simply Sheol (see New American Standard Bible). People of the Old Testament believed that the dead continued existence in the dreary underworld of Sheol. It was not until later that Sheol was conceived of as being divided into two compartments where good dwelt and where evil dwelt.

The most prominent Greek word translated "hell" is *gehenna*. Jesus used the word eleven times (Matt. 5:22, 29, 30; 10:28; 18:9; 23:15, 33; Mark 9:43, 45, 47; Luke 12:5). The only other appearance of *gehenna* is in James 3:6 where he described hell as the source of the evil of an uncontrolled tongue. Neither Paul, Peter, nor John used the word in their writings. *Gehenna* is a transliteration of the Hebrew words *ge* and *hinnom*. This was the name for the "Valley of Hinnom" located southeast of the city of Jerusalem. The word *hinnom* came from the Hebrew word meaning "lamentation." During the days of Ahaz and Manasseh, some Jews erected a temple to the Canaanite fire god, Molech (Jer. 7:31). Worshiping Molech included putting a baby in the arms of a heated idol and burning it to death. This brought screams from the babies and wailings from the mothers, thus the place received its name.

Josiah, king of Judah, destroyed the temple and forbade worship of Molech. The Valley of Hinnom afterwards became a despised place to the Jews. They abhorred the previous practices of child sacrifice to the Canaanite deity. The place became so despised that people dumped their trash in the valley. Fires had to be kept burning continuously to keep the place sanitary. *Gehenna* offered a way to express the idea of the eternal destruction of the wicked. It came to be a term used to present the idea of something abominable.

Another Greek word translated hell is *hades.* It comes from *hades* the Greek infinitive *idein,* meaning "to see." The form of the word used here is stated as a negative, meaning "not to see." Therefore, *hades* means "the unseen world." The word was used to mean the same as the Old Testament word *Sheol,* or "the unseen world of the dead." The word *hades* is translated "hell" eleven times in the King James Version of the New Testament. In five places *hades* seemed to be used as a general reference to the dead (Acts 2:27, 31; where the O.T. reference to "Sheol" is rendered "hades" 1 Cor. 15:55; Rev. 1:18; 6:8). In two verses *hades* referred to the place of the departed wicked (Luke 16:23; Rev. 20:13, 14). Then it was used four times as a general reference to death (Matt. 11:23; 16:18; Luke 10:15; Rev. 20:13).

The other Greek word translated "hell" in the New *tartarus* Testament is *tartarus.* It is used only one time in 2 Peter 2:4. "For if God spared not the angels that sinned, but cast them down to hell, and delivered them into chains of darkness, to be reserved unto judgment...." Plato used the word to identify the place where the incorrigibly corrupt are eternally confined. The word *hell* in this verse is a translation of *tartarus* which is the Roman and Greek equivalent of the concept of *gehenna.* According to Thayer's lexicon, it had the same meaning for the Greeks that *gehenna* had for the Jews. It denoted the subterranean region where evil people go when they die. In apocalyptic literature of the intertestament period, the word was used as a place reserved for the fallen angels.

OLD TESTAMENT TEACHING

Though the Old Testament does not have a clearly defined concept of the life beyond, it does clearly teach of a life after death. It spoke of the dead being in Sheol, meaning sometimes simply "the grave" and other times referring to a place for the departed dead, but often to a dreary fate. Certain passages here and there in the Old Testament suggest possibilities of a better life beyond death for the believer, as in Daniel 12:2. A few Old Testament references seem to differentiate between the lot of the unbelievers and the believers. Reading about the moral teaching of the Old Testament with its strong belief in reward and punishment does not surprise us when we learn that writers during the intertestament period developed further the doctrine of individual destiny. In Jewish writings just before the New Testament period there was a clearly defined doctrine of eternal punishment.

God showed to the prophets some hints of the future punishment of the wicked. Isaiah spoke of those who rebelled against the Lord: "And they shall go forth, and look upon the carcases of the men that have transgressed against me: for their worm shall not die, neither shall their fire be quenched; and they shall be an abhorring unto all flesh" (Isa. 66:24). Most conservative Old Testament scholars believe that this refers to the future punishment of the wicked. Jesus himself used two of these expressions when he taught about the fate of the unbelievers.

Daniel said, "And many of them that sleep in the dust of the earth shall awake, some to everlasting life, and some to shame and everlasting contempt" (Dan. 12:2). Many references in the Wisdom Literature of the Old Testament speak of a terrible fate for the wicked. "The way of the ungodly shall perish" (Psa. 1:6). "For God shall bring every work into judgment, with every secret thing, whether it be good, or whether it be evil" (Eccl. 12:14).

The Old Testament says often that the righteous will be rewarded and that unbelievers will be punished. Though the Old Testament writers spoke to the present, the future to them meant a prolongation of the present. Therefore, if one lived without God during the days of the Old Testament, they would do so also beyond death. The Old Testament gives a hint that death does not destroy the personality. The beliefs in the Old Testament led to the later expression of the ideas of blessedness for the righteous dead and punishment for the unrighteous.

NEW TESTAMENT TEACHING

When we turn to the New Testament, we find many
mentions of hell. We cannot help but notice that Jesus had
more to say about hell than did any other person. It appears
that the strongest support for a real hell comes from him.
Neither the early church nor the first apostles invented hell.
They simply affirmed Christ's teaching about it.

Matthew recorded the teachings of Christ, so it is in
Matthew that we see much of Jesus' ideas on hell. Jesus spoke
about the evil of hatred and the lustful look. "But I say unto
you, That whosoever is angry with his brother without a
cause shall be in danger of the judgment: and whosoever shall
say to his brother, Raca, shall be in danger of the council:
but whosoever shall say, Thou foul, shall be in danger of hell
fire" (Matt. 5:22). "And if thy right eye offend thee, pluck
it out, and cast it from thee: for it is profitable for thee that
one of thy members should perish, and not that thy whole
body should be cast into hell. And if thy right hand offend
thee, cut it off, and cast it from thee: for it is profitable for
thee that one of thy members should perish, and not that thy
whole body should be cast into hell" (Matt. 5:29, 30).

Jesus spoke of hell in several of his parables. In the parable
of the wheat and tares, he said, "As therefore the tares are
gathered and burned in the fire; so shall it be in the end of this
world. The Son of man shall send forth his angels, and they
shall gather out of his kingdom all things that offend, and
them which do iniquity; and shall cast them into a furnace of
fire: there shall be wailing and gnashing of teeth" (Matt.
13:40-42). Also, in the parable of the net Jesus spoke of the
anguish of the unsaved with identical words (Matt. 13:49, 50).
In the parable of the wedding feast Jesus spoke of exclusion,
outer darkness, and deep remorse (Matt. 22:13). Then in Luke
16:19-31 Jesus, in talking about the rich man and Lazarus,
depicted a terrible, hopeless state for the wicked after death.

Jesus used many metaphors to represent hell. He spoke of
hell as endless torment: "Where their worm dieth not, and
the fire is not quenched" (Mark 9:44). He spoke of hell as
a place of burning fire. "Rather fear him which is able to
destroy both soul and body in hell" (gehenna, Matt. 10:28).
To describe the torment of the place, Jesus said, "There

shall be wailing and gnashing of teeth" (Matt. 13:42). Jesus' use of the metaphorical language does not lessen the horror. It describes a real place of pain much greater than the figures present.

Jesus warned people against hell. He warned the apostles to fear those who could "destroy both body and soul in hell" (Matt. 10:28). He cautioned people to fear a place of loss that was greater than losing an eye or a hand (Matt. 18:8, 9). Jesus would not have warned against an unreal place or existence.

Jesus taught two final destinies for mankind: heaven and hell. He spoke of the future state of the wicked as painful and endless. The worst part of the punishment is that Jesus will not be there. Before anyone denies that hell is real he should read Christ's words about hell in the four Gospel narratives.

Elsewhere in the New Testament we find other writers who speak about hell. Paul wrote: "In flaming fire taking vengeance on them that know not God, and that obey not the gospel of our Lord Jesus Christ: Who shall be punished with everlasting destruction from the presence of the Lord, and from the glory of his power" (2 Thes. 1:8, 9). Notice how Paul supported Jesus' idea of hell as punishment and separation.

The writer of Hebrews spoke of God's judgment on sin. "Vengeance belongeth unto me, I will recompense, saith the Lord. And again, The Lord shall judge his people. It is a fearful thing to fall into the hands of the living God" (Heb. 10:30, 31). Peter wrote of eternal punishment with graphic language. "For if God spared not the angels that sinned, but cast them down to hell, and delivered them into chains of darkness, to be reserved unto judgment . . ." (2 Pet. 2:4). Peter spoke of the "chains of darkness" suggesting confinement in hell not so much by material bond but as a total loss of dimension, purpose, and meaning of life. This is closely akin to Jesus' idea of "losing your soul." In the Revelation of Jesus Christ, John spoke frequently about hell. In chapter 20 he called hell a "bottomless pit," and "a lake of fire and brimstone." He also said that those in hell would be "tormented day and night forever and ever." He spoke of the experience of hell as "the second death."

These passages from the first-century inspired letters are

proof that the apostles followed their Master in speaking about hell. They spoke of a judgment on sin where the lost suffer the awful results of their sins. They talk about hell as being endless. The New Testament writers were reserved in how they spoke of the nature of punishment compared to what many people today say about hell. The entire New Testament shows that hell is quite real and should be avoided at all costs.

Not everyone who believes in hell or eternal punishment is naive or uninformed about the Bible. One can accept freely what others have said about hell, such as Irenaeus and Polycarp of the second century; Augustine of the fourth century; Thomas Aquinus of the thirteenth century; Martin Luther and John Calvin of the sixteenth century; Jeremy Taylor and Richard Baxter of the seventeenth century; John and Charles Wesley of the eighteenth century; Charles Haddon Spurgeon and D. L. Moody of the nineteenth century; and Billy Graham, W. A. Criswell, H. H. Hobbs, John Sutherland Bonnell, and Leslie H. Woodson of the twentieth century. Many others could be named who believe the Bible declares that hell is real.

DEDUCTIONS

Most serious Bible students want to know why there needs to be a hell and what kind of place hell is. Now that we have shown that the Bible teaches its reality, we can proceed to make other statements about hell. The Bible writers were not "flag wavers" or "pulpit pounders" who merely declared— "There is a hell! There is a hell!" They spoke of sin's consequences. The final payment for sin is hell. To describe the nature of hell, the Bible used picture language and profound words to tell what life in hell is like.

Hell must be taken seriously if we believe in human freedom. There must be a hell to ensure the triumph of justice and defeat of the wicked. It saves a person from being forced to be godly and to live under pressure before the Lord. There must be a hell to allow man to rebel against God. The Lord allows hell to exist so that people may continue in their selfish ways. Hell, therefore, is necessary if one is to have freedom to continue a self-centered existence apart from God.

From reading the Bible several deductions can be made about the nature of hell. The Lord spoke of hell as the ultimate consequence of sin, the loss of all good, and banishment from God's presence. These will be both physical and spiritual experiences. Our Lord spoke of people in hell keeping their earthly identity and being aware of their torment and pain. When Jesus used such language as "unquenchable fire" and "worm not dying," he conveyed that hell is endless.

We can deduce from the Bible that hell means the final result of sin. The New Testament says: "The wages of sin is death" (Rom. 6:23). This is what is meant also by such expressions as "destruction" (Phil. 3:19); "everlasting contempt" (Dan. 12:2); "punishment" (Matt. 25:46); "the wrath to come" (Luke 3:7); "condemnation" (Rom. 8:1); and "recompense" (Heb. 10:30). Many reasons can be given for why sin must be punished. Some say God must vindicate divine righteousness. Others think that punishment will reform sinners. Some even think that punishment will keep people from further sinning. Actually, punishment of sin comes in relation to God's moral design of man and the holiness of God.

God made man in such a way that the laws of nature and moral laws are for man's highest good. When man obeys the moral order, he experiences happiness. But when man rebels against God's intention, true harmony of life is destroyed and the way is opened to show the consequences of rebellion against God. Hell then means to reap the final effect of sin. God made the universe in such a way that the soul that sins must die. Hell is what happens to those who refuse to respond to God's grace. God wants to rescue man from the effects of his sin and save him from the penalty of it.

Not only does man go against the moral makeup of his own nature, but he rebels against the holiness of God. In the Bible, we find that God always reacts against sin. His nature is such that sinful man cannot enter into his presence. God wants to make man holy, but when man does not allow God to enter his life, God has no other choice, because of his holy nature, but to allow man to die—even though it is not what God desired for him.

Death does not end anyone's identity or consciousness. Hell means that one has declared for his life that he chose to live apart from God. This is why hell is forever. God allows a person to make his choice to live apart from him as long as the person wishes. So after death man keeps on living the way he chose. The Bible does not mention death as the end of life. The tendency of sin is to cause us to get further from God. A self-centered person tends to become more self-centered.

From reading other Scriptures, we can deduce that hell means the loss of all good. God has given man a good world. Think of the many good things of life. God gave us light, love, purpose, beauty, happiness, and hope. But hell means the loss of all good things. Such terms as "perish" (John 3:16), "eternal destruction" (2 Thes. 1:8), and other expressions teach us that hell is a tragic loss of everything that is good.

Every person who goes to hell gets what he asks for. During the earthly life the unsaved said, "Not thy will, O God, but mine be done. Not thy love, not thy purposes for me, not thy realm, not thy thoughts, not thy wisdom, not thy laws, not thy life and presence and beauty—but me. Let me be the center of my life!" God allows people to go where they choose to go. Turning from the light of God's goodness, people choose to enter the realm of darkness. This is why the Bible speaks of hell as "outer darkness" (Matt. 22:13), which means an existence bereft of all good which God gave.

Our Lord spoke of being in hell as a great loss. He said, "For what is a man profited, if he shall gain the whole world, and lose his own soul?" (Matt. 16:26). He evidently meant the loss of true life. A person without Christ is spiritually dead in trespasses and sins, and unless he is quickened, made alive by a creative act of the Lord, he will remain dead. To be made alive is to be restored to communion with God. According to the Bible, the wicked dead will be bodily raised. They will retain their personality with its intellect, emotions, memory, and self-consciousness, but they will be spiritually dead. Aware of being separated from God forever will bring enormous torment. There seems to be no possibility of intellectual advancement in this state, for the mind will be haunted by the absence of light.

Clearly enough, the Bible speaks of both a physical and spiritual torment in hell. The Bible does allow for bodily torment though many of us have reacted against gross physical descriptions of hell in current literature. The worst anguish is always spiritual. "Think'st thou," says Marlowe's Mephistopheles, "that I who saw the face of God./ And tasted the eternal joys of Heaven./ Am not tormented with the thousand hells./ In being depriv'd of everlasting bliss?" No greater anguish can come to an individual than to lose real life, the life which God intended.

The worst description which we could give about hell is that it is banishment from the Lord. We wish that this were not true, but the Bible speaks of hell as separation from God. "Depart from me" (Matt. 25:41). The wicked will "go away" (Matt. 25:46). They will be "thrust out" (Luke 13:28). They will go "from the presence of the Lord and the glory of his power" (2 Thes. 1:9). The Christian lives in the presence, knowledge, and fellowship of the Lord. But the unsaved live apart from him.

No one can fully conceive the meaning of being separated from God, for no one on earth has ever been without him. We have never been apart from his love, his concern, his passion for our highest good and our redemption. Even the most wicked person has been under the close supervision of God. Many people know that God knows where a sparrow falls and that the very hairs of our head are numbered. But in hell God puts the wicked out of his mind. Could this have been what the psalmist thought about when he wrote: "Free among the dead, like the slain that lie in the grave, whom thou rememberest no more: and they are cut off from thy hand" (Psa. 88:5). Thinking about being forever shut out from the presence of God and from the mind of God strikes extreme terror.

One can read the Scriptures carefully about what God gives every person in Christ. One can learn that God's Spirit resides in every believer, giving a new being, daily illumination, meaning for life, and a dynamic power to master difficult circumstances. One can read about what God promises the Christian for the future. After reading and studying the Bible from this perspective, one can see the negative side of this teaching, what will happen to those who are not in Christ. Real life is *in Christ*, a life full and meaningful. But *outside of Christ* one has not real life, but an empty and meaningless existence. God promises each believer the blessings of his intimate fellowship. But to the unsaved person God warns about going to eternal punishment and tragic banishment from God's presence.

There awaits an experience and a destiny for a person who chooses to live apart from God. According to the Bible, hell begins the moment one rebels against God. It continues forever with selfish torment and Godless existence.

TWO
PEOPLE THINK DIFFERENTLY ABOUT HELL

Our world is a kaleidoscope of religious thoughts. The diversity of opinions are seen especially with the many interpretations of Scripture which have to do with future punishment. With the same Bible people read and study passages, but they arrive at different opinions about hell.

Opinions about hell resemble those of the blind men of Indostan who, in the well-known poem, make an investigation of an elephant. Six different men examine the same elephant but give different descriptions of what he must be like. People read the same verses, but they view hell differently.

Some say there is no hell. Others say that hell exists only for a brief time. Many have viewed hell with an extremely imaginative mind. The traditional view of hell, simply stated, is that unbelievers suffer endless eternal separation from God.

What view of hell is correct? Some people who deny that hell is real sound very authoritative. Some of their arguments are very convincing.

To get the complete picture about hell we must study the biblical references and pray for God's guidance. It may help to investigate the opinions of other people. Listening and learning how other people view hell does not require an endorsement. The fact that some people arrive at the conclusion that everyone will ultimately be saved should not shatter our faith. None of us is free from our own deep-seated beliefs of hell. Nonetheless, we should look at the opinions of others, not necessarily to promote their views but to learn what we can. Actually, no study of hell would be complete if one studied only the traditional view.

IMAGINATION

The Bible uses vivid language to describe hell. Some of the metaphors used by these first-century writers gave clear pictures. Several words having to do with fire were used: flames, eternal fire, *gehenna*, furnace, fire and brimstone, and the lake of fire. Other metaphors such as gnawing worm, eternal shame, weeping and gnashing of teeth, and darkness depicted the life apart from God. In addition to the metaphors, the Bible employs strong words such as condemnation, perish, and punishment to describe the present and future state of the unsaved. People through the years have often abused the biblical language. Grotesque descriptions have been made about hell where the writers have tried to describe the realities behind the language, with descriptions that depart from the original biblical interpretation.

Through the years hell has often been discussed in literature. *The Divine Comedy* furnished evidence for Dante's wide knowledge of the Bible, the Christian classics, science, history, and Italian politics.

One of Dante's main themes in *The Divine Comedy* was life after death. He divided the future life into the *Inferno* (hell); the *Purgatorio* (purgatory); and the *Paradiso* (paradise). The work is called a *commedia* (comedy) because it ended happily. The section on hell begins the poem. Dante pictured himself as lost in a dark forest. One Good Friday, after a night of painful wandering, Dante met Virgil, the Roman poet. Virgil promised to lead him out of the dark forest. The two reach hell, which was depicted as a horrible pit shaped like a cone, deep in the earth. It had nine circles where Dante and Virgil visited crowds of suffering individuals tormented by monsters and devils. Dante observes closely the damned. He recognized some of the inhabitants of hell from the past and some contemporaries. At this point Dante described hell vividly as a place of enormous physical suffering:

But all those spirits, so forworn and stark,
  Change color, and their teeth are chattering,
  As soon as they the cruel accents mark.
God they blaspheme, and their own sires, and fling
  Curses on race and place and time and taw
  Both of their birth and their engendering.

And now the notes of woe begun to smite
  The hollow of mine ear; now am I come
  Where I am pierced by wailings infinite.
I came into a place of all light dumb,
  Which bellows like a sea where thunders roll
  And counter winds contend for masterdom.
The infernal hurricane beyond control
  Sweeps on and on with ravishment malign
  Whirling and buffering each hapless soul.
When by the headlong and tempest hurled supine,
  Here are the shrieks, the moaning, the laments;
  Here they blaspheme the puissance divine.''

Dante's descriptions seem to be overly-exaggerated. Though the Bible speaks of suffering in hell, it does not necessarily warrant descriptions like Dante's. *The Divine Comedy* ranks as superb literature. Perhaps the poem says more on how Dante felt about Italian politics, for which the poem furnishes a good resource for learning. It depicts Dante's dislike for political corruption. It also records his relentless search for meaning of life. Yet one must realize that the way he described hell is more imaginative than biblical.

Later, the French artist, Paul Gustave Doré pictured Dante's concepts of hell with imaginative drawings. They are excellent works of art, but they are not good resources for a biblical view of hell.

John Milton, an English poet and political writer, wrote the epic *Paradise Lost* during his blindness. Milton was a

deeply religious Puritan. He studied the Bible faithfully.
Paradise Lost describes the sin of Adam and Eve and their
expulsion from the Garden of Eden. It also includes
descriptions of Lucifer's rebellion and fall from heaven to
hell. Milton vividly described Satan and his mighty hosts'
fall into a burning hell. He depicted the agony of the
inhabitants as they loathe the horror of the fiery flames.
Milton without question had a gift of writing that helped
him describe the human predicament. He was prophetic of
sin's consequences. Yet, we must remember that *Paradise
Lost* was a seventeenth-century poetical work, which
contains lengthy verbal embellishments of the conflict
between good and evil. Though it reflects on what the
Bible says about hell, one must be careful not to accept this
poem as an inspired description of hell. It ranks as good
literature but *not* as a biblical commentary on hell.

Theologians, especially during the intertestament period
and the Middle Ages, gave elaborate descriptions of physical
torture. *The Apocalypse of Peter*, written during the early
Christian era, described the wicked "hanging by their
tongues, while the flaming fire torments them from
beneath." It spoke of women hanging by their hair over the
bubbling mire, "because they adorned themselves to
adultery." The murderers were pictured as thrown into "a
pit full of evil reptiles."

In the Middle Ages, Thomas Aquinas (1225-1274), the
famous Roman Catholic theologian, said, "Wherefore in
order that the happiness of the saints may be more delightful
to them and that they may render more copious thanks to
God for it, they are allowed to see perfectly the sufferings
of the damned."

Richard de Hampole (1290-1349), an English mystic,
devoted a thousand lines in *Stimulus Conscientiae* to the
torments of hell. Even the gentle Francis of Assisi thanked
God that the accursed ones would be sent to hell. Queen
("Bloody") Mary of England desired the souls of heretics
to be burned in the flames of hell.

Such descriptions of hell are not limited to the Middle
Ages. The nineteenth-century Roman Catholic priest, Father
Furness, described eternal punishment: "The little child is

in this red-hot oven. Hear how it screams to come out. See
how it turns and twists itself about in the fire. It hurts its
head against the roof of the oven. It stamps its little feet on
the floor of the oven."[1] Some twentieth-century writers
and orators describe vividly the physical torture of hell. One
went so far as to give the exact Fahrenheit degrees of hell.

At times evangelical preachers have used vivid imagination
to describe hell. Jonathan Edwards, in his eighteenth-century
sermon, described hell as a great furnace. He sought to
get his listeners to imagine touching the coals of the hot
furnace. Edwards described an angry God holding the damned
over a lake of fire and brimstone as one would a spider over
a fire.

A preacher once turned out the lights in the sanctuary.
Lighting a torch, he walked up and down the aisles asking
people to feel the hotness of the fire. Needless to say, the
sermon made quite an impression. But how can anyone
honestly say that this really presents the New Testament
doctrine of hell? It seems to be an exaggerated emphasis on
the physical. The physical description of hell need not be
eliminated from sermons, but an emphasis on the spiritual
would be far more biblical.

Many of us acquired our beliefs about hell from so-called
"hell-fire and damnation preaching," from which comes a
concept of hell that speaks mainly of physical torture. The
abode of the unsaved appeared something akin to the brick
kilns in my home town which I passed almost every day.
When I went by them, I viewed the glowing flames and felt
the intense heat. I imagined that hell must be like that.
Further study of God's Word taught me that this concept was
probably not accurate. Like many evangelical sermons
dealing with hell, this view caused me to spend too much
time with the physical aspect of hell. It made me neglect the
spiritual suffering of remorse, misery, intense evil, and
separation from God as well as many other spiritual losses
the unsaved suffer.

None of the recorded sermons in the New Testament
describe hell imaginatively. The apostles mentioned the
ultimate fate of the wicked, but they did not try to describe
hell. Peter urged people to be saved. Paul urged people to

repent in view of God's final judgment. Apostolic sermons described life in two directions: life in Christ and life outside of Christ. Living in Christ means a joyous life on earth and a blessed eternity. Life outside of Christ produces misery both now and forever.

Whether the biblical language about hell should be interpreted as literal or symbolic seems to be a side issue. The main concern should be whether one takes hell seriously. Hell can be presented with such terms as loneliness, meaninglessness, hopelessness, remorse, regret, self-loathing, envy, malice, ill-will, hostility, hatred. This seems to be the truth about hell which the Bible writers sought to give.

RESTORATIONISM

Some serious-minded Bible students conclude that eventually every person will be saved, a view which is called universalism. It is the view that an opportunity for salvation will be possible beyond the grave. One of the earliest proponents of this view was Origen, an outstanding third-century churchman. He advocated that the punishments of the condemned are not endless, but remedial. Many theologians, such as Emil Brunner, find this view attractive. Brunner wrote: "One must believe in eternal punishment to fear God and universal salvation to love God."[2]

Restorationism takes several forms. One view is that death produces a change of character, a view held by very few Bible students today. Another view of restorationism holds that those who die without hearing the gospel receive another chance. Using 1 Peter 3:19 as their proof text, they say that Christ preaches to the disembodied spirits of the unsaved after their death. The probation period ends at the final judgment day. A third view, the most popular form today, maintains that suffering leads people to turn from their sins. They advocate that God uses the strong and stern sufferings of hell to turn people to him.

People get the idea of a second chance from misinterpreted Scripture. They also use inferences from God's nature and the moral universe. Just as the blind men got a picture of an elephant from a partial examination, so the universalists get an incomplete picture of hell. Looking at some of the Scripture used to support restorationism is helpful.

Restorationists cite, for example, Acts 3:21; Ephesians 1:10; 1 Corinthians 15:22; 1 Timothy 2:4; and 4:10 to make their point.

Acts 3:21 says, "Whom the heaven must receive until the times of restitution of all things, which God hath spoken by the mouth of all his holy prophets since the world began." Some say that the expression "restitution of all things" refers to a universal expectation. Those who hold this view ignore the two verses further in Acts 3:23 where Peter spoke of some people being destroyed. "And it shall come to pass, that every soul, which will not hear the prophet, shall be destroyed from among the people."

Ephesians 1:10 says, "That in the dispensation of the fulness of times he might gather together in one all things in Christ, both which are in heaven, and which are on earth; even in him." The passage refers to the entire universe rather than to individuals. Jesus is presented as the unifying bond of all things. God will one day bring all things together in Christ. The verse doesn't teach necessarily that all people will be saved, but that opposition and disharmony will be ended.

Perhaps the favorite passage of restorationists is 1 Corinthians 15:22: "For as in Adam all die, even so in Christ shall all be made alive." Grammatically the word *all* refers to the ones about whom he is speaking, namely the believers in Christ. Paul discussed the resurrection, not the reception of life from Christ. The verse analyzes the relation between Christ and his followers and Adam and his descendants.

The two passages in 1 Timothy in 2:4 and 4:10 express God's desire for all mankind. "Who will have [desires] all men to be saved and to come unto the knowledge of the truth" (2:4); "For therefore we both labour and suffer reproach because we trust in the living God, who is the Saviour of all men, specially of those that believe" (4:10). The fact that God desires the salvation of every person does not mean all will be saved. The second passage clearly states that God is "the Saviour of all men, specially of them that believe."

God wants everyone to have eternal life, but whether we receive it is left up to us.

In addition to citing the Bible, the restorationists also use human reasoning. They argue along three lines. First, they present the fact that God is love and his love could never rest content with people suffering in hell. The argument does sound logical, but it does not account for either God's holiness and justice nor his expressed desire to bless us. God deals with people as moral beings, responsible and free. Eternal punishment is the result of man's sin.

Second, restorationists argue that no condition of man is permanent. Since man is free, his freedom must mean an indeterminate will. In other words, they contend that if man does not like hell, he can change. This infers that future sufferings will lead the sinner to choose God. This view also sounds logical, but is misleading, because a person can respond only to the light he has been given. Oftentimes the reasoning powers are deeply convicted, but the will of man continues to resist. To be sure, hell will convince man of the Lord God, but the choice will not be given him beyond this life.

Third, restorationists reason that hell violated God's kingdom. They believe that everlasting hell involves a dualism of good and bad. Therefore, some say that a holy and loving God will seek to abolish hell in the interest of unity. It is true the problem of evil's presence now creates a problem for people from an earthly standpoint, but nowhere does the Bible support the idea that evil and God will ever be reconciled.

Restorationism appeals to people. The thought that every person will go to heaven strikes a responsive chord. But the words of Jesus in Matthew 25:46 expressly contradict universalism. Speaking of the unsaved, Jesus clearly stated, "These shall go away into everlasting punishment." In another place, Jesus spoke of the impassable gulf between the saved and unsaved after death (Luke 16:19-31).

One of the most serious faults of universalism is that it violates human freedom. The Bible clearly teaches that God respects a person's right to choose. God cannot make bad people happy. They must renounce sin by their own choice.

People cannot be forced to be holy. It must be chosen. Hell is, in one sense, a monument to man's selfishness and disobedience.

Closely akin to restorationism is the Roman Catholic idea of purgatory. Through the years Roman Catholics believed in three places for the departed: heaven, hell, and purgatory. Thomas Aquinas said that the wicked pass immediately to hell, which is endless, and from which there is no release. Those who made fullness of grace offered in the church go immediately to heaven. The majority of Christians who have imperfectly availed themselves of grace undergo a long or short period of purification in purgatory. Roman Catholics never contend in their idea of purgatory that all men will finally be saved.

But some Protestant groups substitute an idea of purgatory for hell. Carl F. H. Henry says that among many modern theologians hell is being transferred into a "new-Protestant purgatory."[3] To be thoroughly biblical, one needs to admit that one of two fates await people at their death. The unsaved go to hell. The saved enter into heaven.

ANNIHILATIONISM

A few serious Bible students believe that the soul is not itself immortal. They believe that the unsaved do not exist beyond the grave. Thus, annihilationists do not believe in hell. According to their view, a person becomes immortal by faith in Christ. When they unite with Christ, the soul is made immortal by the Holy Spirit. These ideas are some-times labeled as "conditional immortality." Outside of a union with Christ, the soul deteriorates and finally is annihilated.

There are different views within annihilationism. One view holds that at death every unsaved person ceases to exist. Another form claims that annihilation does not come immediately. According to this view, the unsaved remain in hell in a conscious state until the day of judgment. After judgment they cease to exist. This view allows time for the suffering of the full penalty of sins.

Again you might wonder where people get such ideas.

Actually the source of it is Greek philosophy. The Platonists taught that man is not immortal by birth. Platonists believe that good is real, and evil does not exist. Therefore, there remains no room for everlasting death. Using the speculation of Platonism, some contend that God and good continue forever, but Satan and evil will be completely annihilated. From the Platonic philosophy, the annihilationist says that man is a creature with no natural immortality. Man, according to annihilationists, becomes eternal only on the basis of faith in Christ. This would mean that death means cessation of being for the unsaved.

To support their view, annihilationists use the Bible. They quote verses which contain the words death, destruction, perdition, abolishing, perishing, and loss. On the surface this sounds as if the Bible does teach total destruction. Some words which the annihilationists claim for cessation of existence are used to mean something far different. To understand their argument we need to look at the Scripture passages they quote. They use Isaiah 57:1: "The righteous perisheth." The same Hebrew word (abadh) means lost as in 1 Samuel 9:3, "The asses of Kish Saul's father were lost." Obviously Kish's asses were not annihilated.

Annihilationists claim that the expression "cut off" in Psalm 37:9 means annihilation. Daniel, however, used the same Hebrew word (karath) in 9:26: "And after threescore and two weeks shall Messiah be cut off, but not for himself." Evidently the writer did not predict the annihilation of the Messiah.

Again the annihilationists use the word destroy to support their position. "The wicked will he destroy" (Psa. 145:20). Other Old Testament uses of the word do not mean cessation of being. Hosea said, "O Israel, thou hast destroyed thyself" (13:9), which clearly does not mean annihilation. During the destructive days of the plagues of Egypt, Pharaoh's servants said, "Knowest thou not yet that Egypt is destroyed?" (Ex. 10:7). Of course, Egypt had not been annihilated.

Other uses of the words often cited by the annihilationists defeat their own theory. Neither the Old Testament nor the New Testament can be applied to mean that death or hell

is a cessation of being. Though the Old Testament has little
to say about future life, the dead in Sheol (the realm of
the dead) are not annihilated. They are, in fact, said to be
conscious: "Their worm dieth not, and the fire is not
quenched" (Mark 9:48). "And [they] shall be tormented day
and night for ever and ever" (Rev. 20:10).

Annihilationists take the biblical expression of fire to
describe complete destruction. Since fire destroys, they use
that part of the figure of speech to prove the annihilation
of the wicked. Burning, however, does not annihilate. Instead,
it changes the form of what is burnt. Burnt paper becomes
ashes and gases, but it does not cease to exist.

In the early days of Christianity, people began to talk of
annihilationism. In the latter part of the second century,
Iraeneus presented the idea that the unsaved ceases to exist
after death. Writing in *Against the Heresies*, he claimed
that one who refuses God destroyed his chances of everlasting
continuance. Tatian said that the unregenerate soul "tends
downward towards matter and dies with the flesh." Scholars
through the years have continued to hold to cessation of
being for the unsaved. Nikolai Berdyaev, writing in the early
part of the nineteenth century said, "Hell unquestionably
exists . . . but it . . . is temporal."[4] Berdyaev's position
contends for a period of time for suffering, but the final result
is annihilation. Paul Tillich, a twentieth-century theologian,
said, "The symbol eternal death is more expressive when
interpreted as self-exclusion from eternal life and consequently from being."[5]

Many groups in America believe in annihilationism. The
Seventh-day Adventists and Jehovah's Witnesses are the
most prominent. The Adventists contend that God will in
the end blot out sin and sinners, and that God will establish
a clean universe again. The Jehovah's Witnesses deny that
there is a real hell, believing that man's makeup does not
allow endless punishment. To them death means total
destruction. When they come to the words *Sheol* and *hades*,
they interpret them literally to be the grave. And the fire
of *gehenna* according to their view symbolized annihilation.

Annihilation is simply another vain attempt to reconcile
God's love with eternal punishment. It is understandable

why it is difficult for some to embrace both the severity of
hell and the compassion of Christ. The Bible definitely
says that the righteous will reign with the Lord. But sorrow-
fully, it also declares that the wicked will suffer in hell
endlessly.

ETERNAL SEPARATION

We have looked into some diverse opinions about the
future life of the unsaved. But we haven't yet looked at the
traditional view which is sometimes called the doctrine of
"eternal punishment" or "eternal separation." This view
teaches that those outside of Christ will in the end be
separated from God and his people, and will experience the
suffering which lasts forever.

The traditional view of hell comes from the Bible, from
such expressive metaphors as: "unquenchable fire" (Matt.
3:12), "fire and brimstone" (Rev. 14:10), and "worm dieth
not" (Mark 9:48). For the most part, these figures depict a
greater suffering than the pictures portray. The Bible depicts
both the spiritual and physical aspect of suffering. We can
be sure that the figures fall short of the reality.

In addition to the metaphors, the traditional doctrine of
hell comes from numerous biblical words, such as
"contempt" (Dan. 12:2), "destruction" (2 Thes. 1:9; 2 Pet.
3:7; Rev. 11:18), "punishment" (Matt. 25:46), "damnation"
(2 Pet. 2:3), and "avenger" (1 Thes. 4:6).

The Bible also talks about a separation between the people
of God and those who refuse to be. God will pass final
judgment, and God's people live with him forever. The
unsaved live in exclusion from God's presence (Rev. 22:15;
Matt. 25:41; 2 Pet. 2:14).

The doctrine of eternal separation is clear in the Scriptures.
Rationalistic thinkers should find the doctrine sound also,
since it seems reasonable even by human speculation that
evil should be punished.

Most of the early church fathers did advocate the doctrine
of eternal punishment. Tertullian, the second-century
churchman and father of Latin theologies, spoke of "the
greatness of the punishment which continueth, not for a

long time, but forever." Augustine, a fourth-century churchman, devoted the entire Twenty-First Book of his *City of
God* to the subject of hell.

Most reputable theologians in the Middle Ages taught also
the doctrine of eternal punishment. Even though they
presented punishment with extreme forms, they did
emphasize the seriousness of sin's ultimate consequences.
Some of the views about hell taught during the Middle
Ages were not really biblical. For example, one finds no
support for the belief that saints in heaven rejoice over the
punishment of the damned. Neither is there any mention
in the Bible of the lurid physical descriptions as we discussed
earlier. Eternal punishment as taught during the Middle
Ages had many humanistic embellishments.

Eschatology (a study of last things) was not an important
issue among men of the reformation, but hell did receive
some mention. Martin Luther spoke of hell in a few of his
writings. John Calvin wrote extensively about hell in his
monumental work *Institutes of the Christian Religion.* The
outstanding Catholic theologian of this period was Ignatius
Loyola. His Fifth Exercise in *Spiritual Exercises* described
the sufferings in hell according to the five senses of
seeing, hearing, tasting, touching, and smelling.

Throughout history, churchmen continued to believe in
the idea of eternal separation. One of the greatest British
theologians and pastors of the seventeenth century was
Richard Baxter, who devoted two chapters to the misery of
the unsaved in *The Saints' Everlasting Rest.* E. B. Pusey,
an outstanding nineteenth-century expositor, wrote a
book entitled *What Is of Faith As to Everlasting Punishment*
(1880), a classic in defense of the traditional position of
eternal punishment. Charles Haddon Spurgeon, the great
British Baptist preacher of the nineteenth century, preached
numerous sermons on hell. In one sermon he said, "We
have never seen the invisible things of horror. That land of
terror is a land unknown. God has put somewhere, on the
edge of his dominion, a fearful lake that burneth with fire and
brimstone."[6]

Roman Catholics have not discarded the doctrine of hell
despite their shift in other beliefs following Vatican II.

They continue to teach that punishment in hell is twofold. First, they describe hell as the pain of loss *(poena damni)*, the worst punishment, the deprivation of all good, and the banishment from the vision of God. Second, they describe the pain of senses *(poena sensus)*, which is the punishment of senses. Roman Catholics are not specific as to whether or not they believe that the fire is literal.

John R. W. Stott, of All Soul's Church in London, says: "Hell is a grim and dreadful reality. Let no man deceive you. Jesus himself spoke of it. He often called it 'outer darkness,' because it is infinite separation from God who is light. It is also called in the Bible 'the second death' and 'the lake of fire,' terms which describe (no doubt symbolically) the forfeiture of eternal life and the ghastly thirst of the soul which are involved in irrevocable banishment from God's presence."[7] Helmut Thielicke wrote: "To be in hell simply means to be utterly separated from God, but in such a way that one is compelled to see him, that one must see him as a thirsty man sees a silvery spring from which he dare not drink. This is hell: to be forced to see the glory of God and have no access to it."[8]

Seeing the various views about hell helps us to see the New Testament doctrine of eternal separation more clearly and objectively. There seems to be little doubt that the view of eternal punishment and separation is thoroughly biblical.

The honest person cannot close his or her mind to the clear teachings of God's Word. Failing to look thoroughly and objectively into what the New Testament teaches about hell could result in something like the blind men's description of the elephant.

THREE
THE SERIOUS PICTURES

The divinely inspired Bible writers used the language of their times to describe hell. In many cases, these writers used vivid, descriptive, pictorial language. Such picture language as outer darkness, lake of fire, bottomless pit, impossible gulf, undying worm, and weeping and gnashing of teeth offered spiritual realities about hell. These New Testament pictures based on Eastern settings seem strange to the literal mindset of Western culture. These Eastern writers employed word pictures that communicated the reality of present and future punishment for the unsaved, portraying the explicit nature of eternal punishment.

People over the years have differed in their interpretations of these biblical expressions. Some have interpreted the grotesque physical descriptions with extreme literalism. Others believe that the pictures are only figurative or symbolic expressions. While there are some literal passages about hell in the New Testament, many are intended to be figurative. Each picture gives some particular insight into the hideous reality of hell. We can be sure that whatever the Bible says about hell, it must be taken seriously. We can also be sure that in whatever manner the Bible writers used language, either literal or symbolic, the teachings about hell are extremely serious.

When my two sons first became interested in movies, I

took them to see one of the Walt Disney productions. As the boys grew older, I thought they could graduate from Walt Disney movies to more serious ones. They saw advertisements on television about *The Poseidon Adventure*, and urged me to take them.

Thinking my boys had matured enough to appreciate a more serious movie, we went to a packed theater to see this movie about a ship, the *Poseidon*, making its last voyage. On New Year's Eve the passengers were celebrating in a large ballroom, unaware of an enormous tidal wave headed toward them. Without warning the tidal wave hit the large passenger liner and turned the ship over. The production was very realistic so that one could feel the trauma, see people being thrown across the room, others holding onto pipes; water washing them away. Many hung suspended in midair.

I was surprised that my boys laughed during the tragedy. I told them to be quiet. I said, "This is not a funny movie." Nonetheless, as the catastrophe worsened, the boys laughed harder. People in the theater who had paid to see a serious, award-winning picture turned and looked at us. The boys continued to laugh. Finally I took them to the lobby and gave them a lecture on the seriousness of *The Poseidon Adventure*. I cautioned them not to laugh when they saw people getting hurt. After we went back inside, they continued to giggle. They never could quite grasp the seriousness of the picture.

That incident taught me a valuable lesson. The boys had been accustomed to viewing frivolous Saturday morning cartoons, which pictured people being blown up with dynamite, falling out of airplanes, crashing cars, and other impossible feats. The cartoons were not serious but lighthearted. Certainly the entertaining Walt Disney movies had not prepared them for something more serious. They had seen daring performances of *The Absent Minded Professor* and the spectacular maneuverability of Herbie in *The Love Bug*. I could not really blame them for misunderstanding the seriousness of *The Poseidon Adventure*.

But blame can go to the person who interpets the biblical pictures of hell frivolously. All through the New Testament serious language was used to present spiritual truth. For example, Jesus often used picture language. He spoke of himself as the Vine, the Bread of life, the Light of the world, the Good Shepherd, the Door, and many other figurative expressions. He compared the relation of people with him as branches. From the symbols we discover the truth they convey.

To understand the New Testament doctrine of hell we must learn something of the setting of the figures of speech used to describe it. An examination of the metaphorical languages leads one to conclude that the writers were saying that hell is a place of wastefulness, hopelessness, sinfulness, loneliness, and endlessness.

WASTEFULNESS

Several biblical pictures show hell to be a place of wastefulness. The picture of the garbage dump was one of them. The common word which Jesus used for hell was *gehenna*, referring to the Valley of Hinnom located just outside the walls of Jerusalem where Israel and her unfaithful kings burned their sons and daughters in honor of Molech. Gradually the Valley of Hinnom became the garbage dump for the city of Jerusalem.

Evidently the sight of a burning flame and the cast-off filth of the city provided Jesus with an illustration for the ultimate results of evil.

Other New Testament references to fire seem to be closely akin to Jesus' use of *gehenna*. No other descriptive terms have been used to describe hell as frequently as fire. The New Testament writers spoke of it as "fire unquenchable" (Luke 3:17); "everlasting fire, prepared for the devil and his angels" (Matt. 25:41); "the furnace of fire" (Matt. 13:42, 50); "hell fire" (Matt. 18:9), "the lake of fire" (Rev. 19:20; 20:10; 14:15; 21:8); and "fire and brimstone" (Rev. 14:10). Also, in Jesus' story of the rich man and Lazarus, Jesus mentioned "flames" (Luke 16:24).

Many Christians differ on what is meant by "fire," whether it should be interpreted literally or figuratively. Everyone agrees that the serious picture of fire speaks of a place of extreme misery. R. G. Lee once said, "If the fire of hell can be proven to be figurative, hell will be no less unendurable. All who believe they can prove the fire of hell is not literal fire have only removed physical pain, which is the least significant feature of its character. Hell is the madhouse of the universe where remorse and an accusing memory cause unspeakable torture."[1]

As a matter of fact, the figure of fire may mean both a literal and figure picture of eternal punishment. Lee said further, "And if all the terrible language descriptive of hell is figurative, how terrible must be the actuality to which the fingers of all figures point!"[2]

Other references to hell describe conditions associated with the place of refuse where trash is thrown and burned. God gave to every person the precious gift of life, the beautiful universe, and meaningful relationships. He gave every person time, talents, opportunities, and possessions. But man discarded the bountiful gifts of God, making life become a garbage dump. Disobeying God's ideals and laws can make one "a trashy person," life something to be profligated, discarded.

Failure to live according to God's intention destroys life, causing it to be wasted. One Sunday afternoon, a friend and I rushed to a crash scene minutes after an airplane disappeared from the sky. A whole family died in the tragedy. During the afternoon, the Federal Aviation Administration came to the scene to investigate, and for several days they examined the wreckage to find out why the plane crashed. Weeks later, I read a report. The FAA concluded that the inexperienced pilot attempted a maneuver with the craft which the airplane was not built to do. The pilot failed to fly the craft according to the manufacturer's intention.

When people refuse to live according to God's will, they destroy precious life. Hell begins now, starting when one rebels against God's will. Sustained rebellion leads in the end to the garbage dump of eternal wastefulness. No more powerful message about hell can be drawn from the picture of a garbage dump than a wasted life. Hell is filled with people who once were destined to walk with God, but disobedience made them worthless.

When we throw something in the trash can, we consider

it useless. People destined for usefulness in the world have rendered themselves useless. Paul spoke of people who rebelled and that "God gave them up" (Rom. 1:18, 26, 28). Some people choose to destroy themselves. To be without God is to be useless, insignificant.

The garbage dump in the Valley of Hinnom is hard for most of us to visualize since many have never seen or smelled a garbage dump. Jesus' familiar sight of the burning valley depicted the awful reality of sin's ultimate consequences.

HOPELESSNESS

Jesus' story of the ten virgins recorded in Matthew 25:1-12 contains the picture of hopelessness and despair. Marriage feasts in Jesus' day were joyous occasions. The feasts often lasted for several days. According to custom, the bridegroom went to one house while the bridesmaids and bride went to another. The women waited for the groom. The bridegroom decided when the formal ceremony was to be held. Of course the arrangement had been made, but his appearance was at a time of his own choosing.

The ten bridesmaids waiting for the groom had different reactions. Five virgins prepared for the bridegroom's appearance, purchasing plenty of oil, but five virgins failed to prepare. While all the bridesmaids were asleep at midnight, the bridegroom came. They all immediately arose to trim their lamps, but the foolish were unprepared. When they couldn't borrow oil, they went to try to purchase some. When they returned, they said, "Lord, Lord, open to us." Jesus' expression "and the door was shut" portrays the picture of a time when there will be no hope for the unsaved.

In the original setting, the parable told of the Jews' lack of preparation for the Messiah. They resembled the five foolish virgins. Jesus, the long-promised Messiah, came to earth, and Israel was caught unprepared. Many people are also not prepared to meet the Lord in death nor are they ready for his final victorious return to earth. The Bible clearly teaches that the unprepared will have no hope. The door of opportunity will be closed. Nothing is more graphic

or serious than the expression, "And the door was shut"
(Matt. 25:10).

The parable of the rich man and Lazarus in Luke 16:19-31
also spoke of the hopeless despair of hell. Two men lived
in a village. The rich man dressed in "purple and fine linen"
and "fared sumptuously every day." Another man named
Lazarus sat as a beggar at the rich man's gate, waiting for
bread crumbs to be thrown out. Dogs licked at Lazarus' body,
festering with sores. Later in the story both men die, causing
their fortunes to reverse. Lazarus enjoyed heavenly fellowship while the rich man experienced extreme misery in hell.
A number of pictures emerge from the parable. First, there
remained no hope for the rich man to relieve him of his
misery. He begged for relief, but Abraham refused. Second,
there was no possible hope for the rich man to move into
heaven. Jesus spoke of "a great gulf fixed," an impassable
void, depicting the spiritual distance, between the righteous
and the unrighteous.

Several other picture words describe the despair of hell,
such as the expressions, "worm dieth not" (Mark 9:48) and
"unquenchable fire" (Matt. 3:12). No matter how one
interprets these figures, as either figurative or literal, they
describe the hopelessness of hell where misery never ends.

Hell is a place where hope is gone. Hope in the New
Testament is not just wishful thinking, but the confident
certainty based on God's promises. We hope for such things
as a better day, the vindication of righteousness, absence
from trouble, the resurrection from the dead, and the glories
of heaven. Life on earth is made more pleasant by hope.
When we suffer financial setbacks, we hope for a more
prosperous day. When we get sick and pain becomes intense,
we long to get better. Hope brightens our lives and keeps
us going. Hope transforms defeat into anticipated victory.
But to think of having no hope describes well the horror
of hell, where there is no prospect for betterment. People in
hell have lost all possibilities of restoration.

Several years ago off the coast of Massachusetts, the
submarine *S-4* sank, after it had been rammed by another
vessel. Quickly it went to the ocean's floor. The submarine
became a prison for the crew. Rescue ships came as soon

as possible to the scene. Divers went down attempting to
rescue them. As they drew near the vessel, they heard a
tapping from inside. The question was slowly tapped by
Morse code letter by letter: I-S T-H-E-R-E A-N-Y H-O-P-E?
What a welcome message to hear the rescuers say: "There
is hope. We are cutting a way for you to escape." What a
tragedy if the rescuers had to say, "There is no way you
can escape." The men trapped inside would have to consume
the remaining oxygen supply and wait without hope for
rescue.

Waiting for death in a doomed submarine might describe
in a small way what hell is like. The New Testament portrays
hell as a place of utter misery with no relief, no lessening
of frustration, no escape from reality, no chance of improve-
ment.

Paul described life without hope when he wrote to the
Corinthians. He spoke of the possibility of having hope
only in this life. "If in this life only we have hope in Christ,
we are of all men most miserable" (1 Cor. 15:19). It is
common sense to see that, if this world is all there is,
anyone is better off than a Christian.

One of Paul's saddest commentaries on the unsaved
Gentile world was "having no hope, and without God in the
world" (Eph. 2:12). The unsaved Gentile world was filled
with fear and despair. The Greek and Roman world of
Paul's day was a hopeless world.

Anyone without God has to be without hope. People who
seek to live life apart from him are like sailors without
compass or guide who drift on a tempestuous sea in a
rudderless ship on a starless night, far away from the harbor.
Whatever hell might be, the awful hopelessness makes it a
place of utter despair. No more miserable experience could
be conceived. Nothing prevents or lessens the misery in hell.

The rich man mentioned in the Lord's parable chose every
day to be selfish. Opportunities came for him to give, for
Lazarus lay daily at his gate. But the rich man's delayed
decision led to ultimate despair. The five foolish virgins also
learned the penalty of delay. Alfred Lord Tennyson
commented on the parable in verse to Guinevere, the queen.
She discovered too late the high cost of sin.

Late, Late, so late! And dark the night and chill!
Late, late so late! but we can enter still.
Too late, too late! ye cannot enter now.
  No light had we; for that we do repent;
And learning this, the bridegroom will relent.
Too late, too late! ye cannot enter now.
  No light: so late! and dark and chill the night!
O let us in, that we may find the light!
Too late, too late: ye cannot enter now.
  Have we not heard the bridegroom is so sweet?
O let us in, tho' late, to kiss his feet!
No, no, too late! ye cannot enter now.

There can be no sadder sound than the words "too late."

Dante might have exaggerated the biblical pictures of hell in some places. But he described it correctly when he spoke of it as being void of hope. Dante said that the inscription above the portals of hell reads:

When ye step across the sill of hell
Abandon ye all hope.

SINFULNESS

The expressions "outer darkness" and the place where men "weep and gnash their teeth" describe the horror of hell. These expressioins appear six times in Matthew (8:12; 13:42, 50; 22:13; 24:51; 25:30). The Jews used these expressions to describe Sheol. In New Testament times the phrases characterized *gehenna*.

Jesus also used the phrases in Matthew 12:42, 50 to describe the end time. The good and bad coexist together until the harvest day. After the harvest day, the phrases described the unsaved. In Matthew 22:13 Jesus used these thoughts to describe the wedding guest who had not prepared himself.

In the parable of the faithful and unfaithful servants in Matthew 24:45-51, Jesus used the same two expressions. The disobedient servant was punished. He was placed with the hypocrite where there was "weeping and gnashing of

teeth." Again the Lord used the terms in the parable of the
talents in Matthew 25:14-30. He told of a man who left his
servants, one with five talents, another with two, and the
other with one. The servants who had the five and the two
talents multiplied them. The one-talent person hid his talent.
When the master returned, he rebuked the one who had
abused his gift. Jesus said that unfaithfulness was like
rejection of God, and that such servants would be cast into
"the outer darkness" where men weep and gnash their teeth.

These two pictures had reference to *gehenna*. They
describe the consequences of sin. Those who will not trust
the Lord go to hell, and the rejectors of God's righteousness
will be separated from the good. Unprepared people will
be excluded from the festivities of God throughout eternity,
and those who disobey God and choose to live apart from
him are doomed.

The meaning of "outer darkness" is not an unknowable
mystery. Both the Old Testament and New Testament
writers showed the antithesis of good and evil by the symbols
of light and darkness. To describe God's nature they used
the term *light*, and to depict sin and iniquity, they used the
term *darkness*. The psalmist described evil: "Have respect
unto the covenant; for the dark places of the earth are full of
the habitations of cruelty" (Psa. 74:20). Paul said, "For ye
were sometimes darkness, but now are ye light in the Lord:
walk as children of light" (Eph. 5:8). A constant tension exists
between the light and the darkness. Jesus said, "I am the light
of the world: he that followeth me shall not walk in darkness,
but shall have the light of life" (John 8:12). John further
described the conflict: "And the light shineth in darkness;
and the darkness comprehended it not" (John 1:5). Light
represents God, truth, holiness, and life. Darkness stands for
Satan, falsehood, sin, and death. Though darkness and light
constantly battle, light ultimately wins.

Both light and darkness describe the character of people.
First-century Christian writers described people in Christ as
"walking in the light" (1 John 1:7). Everyone and everything
associated with God was expressed in terms of light.
These New Testament writers also described people outside
of Christ as living in darkness (1 John 1:5, 6). The concept

of darkness represents the misery of life apart from Christ now and in the life beyond.

On the earth darkness and light (or good and evil) are mingled. Life on earth is made pleasant and even tolerable by the presence of good. Life's miseries come from the influence and power of darkness. To keep on walking in darkness means an eternity apart from Christ. If one has walked in darkness or lived apart from God, the condition will continue after death. "Outer darkness" is not an optic problem but a sin problem. The human mind can hardly fathom either total light or complete darkness, which is why we cannot understand much about heaven or hell. The inhabitants of hell live in extreme selfishness. Selfishness makes us miserable and uncomfortable. It intensifies our desires, making us grasping, greedy, avaricious, and ravenous throughout our being. It destroys interest in the welfare of others.

The picture of "weeping and gnashing of teeth" is another picture of hell, expressing self-condemnation, self-loathing, and misery. This may well refer to the gnawing pains of self-inflicted anguish eating away at the vitals of the soul. Christianity clearly teaches that after death personality survives. This means that when we leave this earth the only thing we take is ourselves.

LONELINESS
Hell is a place of loneliness. The parable of the rich man and Lazarus gives an insight that the rich man felt all alone. He could see but not enjoy the life of the redeemed. He lived apart from God and Lazarus on earth, and death only intensified his loneliness. On earth he had not treated Lazarus cruelly. He simply failed to notice or help the poor man. Lazarus longed for fellowship. Part of the rich man's anguish in hell was his separation from God and from his people. In addition to other pictures flashed in this parable of the life beyond, the reality of loneliness for the unsaved is certain.

Jesus used the symbol in Luke 13:25-30 of a householder who left his door open, an invitation for anyone to enter. Yet, at an appropriate time, the feast began, and the door was closed, leaving certain sad people knocking and crying, "Lord, Lord, open unto us" (Luke 13:25). Afterwards Jesus said they would be "thrust out" (v. 28). People being lonely and in despair is one of the certain truths about hell.

Man seems to be lonely because he clings tenaciously to his own self-sufficiency. Hell consists of those people who refused to rely upon the Lord. One of T. S. Eliot's characters in *The Cocktail Party* said: "What is hell? Hell is oneself, hell is alone. . . . There is nothing to escape from and nothing to escape to. One is always alone."[3]

Hell involves the intense feelings of being alienated from others, the fear of being different from others, of being cut off from meaningful relationships. Loneliness sounds like what the Bible says about people being lost. They are adrift from life's meaning. In his play, *Orpheus Descending*, Tennessee Williams has one of his characters say a gloomy thing, "We've got to face it, we're under a life-long sentence to solitary confinement inside our lonely skins for as long as we live on this earth!"[4]

Sarah Bernhardt was one of the world's greatest actresses in the early 1900s. She admitted that she played the part of Ophelia hundreds of times before she knew how *Hamlet* ended. Her interest in the play ceased when she performed her part. For those who make self the center of life, hell has already begun.

Aloneness does not make happiness, for the unsaved loathe themselves. Togetherness does not enhance happiness for the unsaved, for other people do not always fit into their selfish demands.

ENDLESSNESS

The New Testament use of the word *gehenna* conveys many messages about the final state of the unsaved. Several insights can be derived from Jesus' words about hell in Mark 9:43-48. Jesus said that everything which imperiled a man's chance for eternal life should be ruthlessly renounced. If the hand offends cut it off. If the foot offends, cut it off. If the eye offends, pluck it out. These are serious words which convey the truth that no sacrifice is too great to gain life in God's kingdom. It means that something dear to us on earth might have to be abandoned. The exclusion might be as painful as cutting off a part of our body. But to know God's kind of life, we must make the choice.

After Jesus spoke of the sacrifice, he talked about hell, using the word *gehenna*. Evidently Jesus referred to the horrible conditions in the valley where loathsome worms bred in the carcasses of dead animals. The place burned, fire smoldered, and smoked continuously like a vast incinerator. The phrases about the worm which does not die and the fire which is not quenched come from a description of the fate of Israel's enemies. "And they shall go forth, and look on the carcasses of the men that have transgressed against me: for their worm shall not die, neither shall their fire be quenched: and they shall be an abhorring unto all flesh" (Isa. 66:24).

Some people seek to explain these figures another way. Since they cannot accept the fact that suffering in hell continues forever, they use various means to explain away the idea of perpetual suffering in hell. Some claim that the term "forever and ever" means a prescribed period of time but not eternal. Looking at many of the ways it is used in the New Testament, however, proves that it must mean always. Jesus Christ on the throne lives "for evermore" (Rev. 1:18). The saints adore the victorious Christ "for ever and ever" (Rev. 5:13). The term is also used to describe suffering. "And her smoke rose up for ever and ever" (Rev. 19:3). "And shall be tormented day and night for ever and ever" (Rev. 20:10). These verses all seem to show that the expression "forever and ever" means just that. One has to be imaginative to derive a prescribed period of time from the phrase "forever and ever."

Other people object to the endlessness of hell by saying that the Greek word *aionios* translated "eternal" means a kind of life. They restrict the usages of the word to a qualitative existence. They consider the word *eternal* to mean only a new kind of life and not duration. The word does mean a kind of existence, and it does sometimes have a qualitative meaning in the New Testament, especially in

John's writings. "And this is life eternal, that they might know thee the only true God, and Jesus Christ, whom thou hast sent" (John 17:3). But to consider the word "eternal" only on the basis of quality misses the original usages of the word.

In classical Greek, the Greek adjective *aionois* meant "perpetual, continual, lasting, unbroken or uninterrupted existence," or "forever." Outside the New Testament the adjective was used in the sense of quantity. James H. Thayer in *A Greek-English Lexicon of the New Testament* says the word in New Testament times also meant "duration." Paul spoke of God without beginning or end in Romans 16:26. The adjective describes God who will never cease to exist. In many other New Testament references such as 2 Peter 1:11 and 2 Timothy 2:10, the word describes a continuous existence. The references prove that *aionois* also meant duration.

Many scholars believe that *aionois* had both a qualitative and quantitative meaning. In other words, it speaks of a kind or quality of life which never ends. E. Y. Mullins said that *aionois* came to mean quality in its later usages, but in most cases it meant duration.[5] Therefore, the word originally had a quantitative meaning. The expression is used twelve times in the Book of Revelation to mean duration. Eight times it refers to the existence of God and his reign. In one reference, it refers to the duration of the righteous. And in three usages it depicts the duration of punishment for the wicked. Whenever *eternal* referred to quality, the sense of duration remained. The word described a kind of existence for both the righteous and the unrighteous. Notice its use in Matthew 25:46. "And these shall go away into everlasting [*aionois*] punishment: but the righteous into life eternal [*aionois*]." The same word described both kinds of life beyond the grave. Therefore, the word *aionois* or "eternal" may be applied either to punishment or to heaven. Both heaven and hell will be forever. If you could reduce the unsaved's duration in hell, you must also reduce the period of the righteous. Unquestionably, the biblical references teach that neither the godly nor the ungodly cease to exist.

Others object to the endless duration of hell saying that the undying worm and the unquenchable fire are only figures of speech. They contend that these expressions teach that the worms finally consume the entire carcass, and the fire ultimately is extinguished. Again, one must not force the pictures. These figures teach the endless nature of hell. To go beyond the intention of the analogy is a mistake.

The torments of hell are hard to accept. The continuous misery is more difficult to accept. But, when we look at the New Testament pictures and read the references, we have no other alternative but to believe that hell is a terrible, terrible place which never ends.

Hell must be understood in terms of the authority of Scripture. Despite what the Bible says, it is always serious when it mentions the final judgment on sin. No matter what picture is used, the reality is far worse than the representation.

Judging from the biblical writers' use of language, one comes to see a serious picture of hell. To argue whether the biblical figures are literal or symbolic is not a legitimate pursuit. We must look beyond the language to the Lord's message about hell. If the biblical teaching about hell is to be understood, the pictorial language needs to be taken seriously.

FOUR
THE ISOLATION WARD

One of the ladies in my church contracted infectious
hepatitis. Her physician placed her in isolation. I visited the
hospital, but was not allowed to enter her room. Several
warning signs were posted: "Absolutely No Visitors,"
"Isolation," "Surgical Dress Required." After several days,
the lady sent word that she needed to see me. Being in
isolation caused her anxiety to increase. She became fearful
and depressed. She felt that a pastoral call might help
her. Her physician agreed that a visit might be helpful.

I drove to the hospital to visit her, where the medical
personnel dressed me in a surgical gown and put rubber
gloves and a surgical mask on me. As soon as the lady saw
me, she smiled and said, "Thank you for coming inside,
pastor. I felt that I had to talk with someone. Physically I
seem to be improving but mentally I don't know. I get
feelings that I am in jail. My friends can't come to see me,
and the longer I stay in the room the more nervous I get."

After listening to her feelings and offering some thought
exercises to more pleasant and positive thinking, I prepared
to leave. We prayed together.

As I turned to walk from the room the lady said, "Preacher,
let me tell you one more thing."

"What's that?" I asked.

"I am not going to hell because I know Jesus, but I know
what hell is like!"

Interested in her statement, I asked, "What do you mean you know what hell is like?"

She then said, "Hell is like an isolation ward. Being shut up with yourself is extremely painful. Being shut away from those you love hurts."

Her insight of being "shut up with herself" and being "shut away from others" made me think more seriously about hell. The Bible does in fact describe hell in terms of separation from God. Jesus said, "Then shall he say also unto them on the left hand, Depart from me, ye cursed, into everlasting fire, prepared for the devil and his angels" (Matt. 25:41). Later in the same story Jesus said, "And these shall go away into everlasting punishment: but the righteous into life eternal" (Matt. 25:46). Luke recorded Jesus' words, "But he shall say, I tell you, I know you not whence ye are; depart from me, all ye workers of iniquity" (Luke 13:27). In another place Jesus said, "But the children of the kingdom shall be cast out into outer darkness: there shall be weeping and gnashing of teeth" (Matt. 8:12). Writing about the abode of the unsaved, the author of Revelation said, "But the fearful, and unbelieving, and the abominable, and murderers, and whoremongers, and sorcerers, and idolaters, and all liars, shall have their part in the lake which burneth with fire and brimstone: which is the second death" (Rev. 21:8). "For without are dogs, and sorcerers, and whoremongers, and murderers, and idolators, and whosoever loveth and maketh a lie" (Rev. 22:15). Then Paul wrote, "Who shall be punished with everlasting destruction from the presence of the Lord, and from the glory of his power" (2 Thes. 1:9). "Depart from me"; "these shall go away"; "their part in the lake of fire"; "cast him out"; "without are dogs"; "from the presence of the Lord"; all of these phrases describe hell as a place of endless suffering and separation from God.

One of the prominent truths in Jesus' story of the rich man and Lazarus is separation. Jesus spoke about a large, impassable gulf dividing the rich man and Lazarus. The rich man was separated from God and from God's people. Hell became a place of isolation for the rich man where he was locked in with himself and away from God and other people. Describing hell as a place of isolation conforms to the nature of sin. Sin begins with disbelief and disobedience of God, as a person asserts his or her rebellion against the Lord God. It involves the exchange of Christ's lordship for the anarchy of human freedom in which every person becomes a tyrant. Whenever we oppose God's will, we break the fellowship with God. To the unsaved, life is completely selfish. Each act of disbelief and disobedience moves one farther from the Lord. Continued rebellion leads to final separation. People can lock themselves out from the intimacy with God, but by doing so they fasten themselves in the straitjacket of their choice and suffocate in selfishness.

Several years after I talked with the lady in the isolation ward, I visited another church member in more intense and longer isolation. A young twenty-nine-year-old man discovered that he had leukemia. He went to one of the finest cancer treatment hospitals in the world, where he received treatment to arrest the increase of white blood cells. For the medication to be effective, he had to be in complete isolation. His food was sterilized. No person could come near him. After over seventy days of isolation, I visited him and talked with him through the partitions. From my extensive conversation with him I learned how he felt about an isolation ward.

How can we describe total isolation? First, it brings inward turmoil, since living alone can be painful. Introspection, while at times helpful, can degenerate into periods of suffering. Isolation alienates us from family and friends. One of life's greatest joys is the presence of other people. To be shut up alone and away from others robs us of that joy. Isolation can cause one to feel separated from God.

INWARD TURMOIL

Hell means to be shut up alone. No words can describe the anguish and torment of being alone with one's self. Those in hell are those who tried to manage life according to their selfish desire. They have exchanged God's generous lordship for the anarchy of human freedom. Consequently, hell contains only selfish people. When death comes to the unsaved, they begin to experience forever the horrible freedom they demanded and become enslaved to their selfish desires.

All of us have some inward conflicts. Disbelief and disobedience of God create serious psychological problems. Everyone suffers some sense of self-estrangement brought on by our sin, since our actions are the outward and visible expressions of our inward sin. Actions come from the heart. The spots a sick person has do not constitute the measles. The spots are only the symptoms of the disease which has invaded the body. Our sins are symptoms, too, revealing that something is wrong within the life.

The inward rebellion within man results in all kinds of sinful actions and attitudes. "That which cometh out of the man, that defileth the man. For from within, out of the heart of men, proceed evil thoughts, adulteries, fornications, murders, thefts, covetousness, wickedness, deceit, lasciviousness, an evil eye, blasphemy, pride, foolishness: all these evil things come from within, and defile the man" (Mark 7:20-23).

Paul also defined the products of a selfish heart, "Now the works of the flesh are manifest, which are these; Adultery, fornication, uncleanness, lasciviousness, idolatry, witchcraft, hatred, variance, emulations, wrath, strife, seditions, heresies, envyings, murders, drunkenness, revellings, and such like" (Gal. 5:19-21). All of the sins which you can think and name originate from one common source—a disbelief and disobedience of God.

Every person on earth has done sinful things and had sinful attitudes. Even the saved are not free from disbelief and disobedience which show up in many kinds of symptoms. But there is a clear difference between the saved and the unsaved. The saved person has opened his life to Jesus Christ. Jesus has forgiven him of his sins. The Holy Spirit lives within each believer, seeking to give the person power over sin. The believer anticipates an eternity completely free from selfishness when he dies. The unsaved person is one who refuses to allow God into his life. God earnestly desires to forgive him and to give him power for victory over self. Yet, he continues to live enslaved to himself and his selfish desires. When the unbeliever dies, he reaps what he wanted.

Since he refused to trust and obey, God abandons him to his selfishness.

Perhaps modern psychiatry could furnish an excellent commentary on the tragic misery caused by disbelief and disobedience. Read again our Lord's words, "From within, out of the heart of men, proceed evil thoughts" (Mark 7:21). He could have been referring to the inward problems of anxiety, fear, despondency, and guilt. Many psychological problems arise from within because of disobedience to God. Disobedience robs one of happiness and often one's mental equilibrium is destroyed. One becomes a battlefield of conflicting thoughts, passions, and desires, and the true harmony of life is destroyed.

Every person on earth has some kind of psychological problem. Some are more serious than others, but no one has complete inward wholeness. Christians can also have anxieties, fear, and guilt, and they also go through periods of depression. But there should be a difference between the believer and the unbeliever in the midst of such inward turmoils. The saved can trust and depend upon the Lord to help bear the burdens or to help break the despondency. The Lord lives within each believer as the Comforter to be alongside and to assist in these feelings. The life to come promises great expectations for Christians. God promises to save them from all anxieties, fears, guilt feelings, and despondency.

The unsaved will not cast their cares on the Lord on earth. Therefore, in their next life they will carry their own intense inward feelings with them forever. They will forever yearn for their conflicts to be resolved. On earth they have soothed these conflicts through various escapes. Perhaps some buried themselves in their work becoming "work-aholics." Others become alcoholics. Many burned in sexual passion and sought to satisfy their God-given desire apart from God's will. In hell every feeling and craving of man has reached its highest intensity, but there will be no possible way in hell to alleviate them. It may be merely a guess, but Jesus could have depicted awful reality of unfulfilled feelings and cravings in the story of the rich man and Lazarus.

The rich man asked frantically, "Father Abraham, have mercy upon me, and send Lazarus, that he may dip the tip of his finger in water, and cool my tongue; for I am tormented in this flame" (Luke 16:24). The rich man found himself in enormous inward turmoil. Added to the turmoil was the inability to be satisfied.

Percy Knauth, a journalist, dealt with the foremost problem of emotional depression in his book *A Season in Hell.* He went through a time of acute mental depression for over one year and a half. He described his emotional depression as "going through hell." Perhaps Knauth was prophetic of the enormity of eternal punishment. If one suffers such terrible anguish in this life that he no longer wants to live, think of how intense and endless those feelings would be in hell itself.

All of us recoil from the thought of a meaningless existence. The Bible teaches that we become our true selves when we submit to God's benevolent lordship. Near the beginning of Augustine's *Confessions,* he said: "Thou has made us for Thyself, and our hearts are restless till they rest in Thee." Man's disbelief and disobedience can cause him to miss the purpose for which God made him. Signs of man's despair about life are all around us. Many today say that life for them has no meaning. These people are often influenced by some of the pagan existential philosophers. They strive to find the mystery of why we are here. Abandoning objectivity and authoritarianism, they strive for subjectivity. A number of dramatists, artists, and musicians talk about man's experience of nonfulfillment. To have no purpose would be one of the worst kinds of life. Though it may sound overly simple, it is nonetheless true that man cannot find meaning for life apart from God.

Both the saved and the unsaved go through frustrating experiences in life. Through the Lord's guidance, the Christian can learn to meet all of these experiences with hope. Sicknesses, sufferings, disappointments, and other troubles can bring despair to Christians. But believers know from the experience of other saints like Job that disaster does not mean defeat. But the unsaved person has no real purpose in life, so it is no surprise that he feels life is meaningless.

Hell is the place of ultimate meaninglessness and frustration over the failure of life itself. In hell the life without significance and meaning continues forever with no way to escape through suicide or self-improvement. This was the reason that the rich man wanted to be released from hell for a while in order to warn his brothers. Not only did he want to warn them of the enormous sufferings of hell, but he wanted to do something at last that had meaning. Everything in hell is futile. It is the empty and meaningless life.

Jean Paul Sartre provides an illustration of meaninglessness in his play *No Exit* with the character Garcin. On earth, Garcin wanted to believe that he was a tough, masculine, heroic type. Garcin said, "I aimed at being a real man, as tough as they say."[1] Contrary to his thoughts about himself, Garcin actually was a coward. Whenever his cowardice threatened to come into his consciousness, he distracted himself by having extramarital sexual affairs. Garcin was not disturbed by these acts, but he disliked feeling that he was a coward.

Fear of conflict led Garcin to become a pacifist newspaper editor. When war erupted, he sought to flee the country but he was captured and shot as a deserter. Sartre's drama continues in hell, where Garcin shares existence with Estelle, a sensuous woman, and Inez, a pervert. In hell Garcin has to face the reality of his life. On earth he had escaped the reality of himself. In hell he tries to escape his true self by making love to Estelle. But Inez continuously reminds him that he is a coward. Garcin, in hell desperately cries, "Will night ever come?"[2] He finds no exit from the awesome reality of himself.

Every person in hell will be destroyed, but it will not mean the destruction of consciousness but of the true self. Listen to Jesus' clear warning, "And fear not them which kill the body, but are not able to kill the soul: but rather fear him which is able to destroy both soul and body in hell" (Matt. 10:28). Soul destruction does not mean annihilation, but destruction of the kind of person that God intended us to be.

It has a kinship to John Greenleaf Whittier's conclusion to "Maud Muller."

For of all sad words of tongue or pen,
The saddest are these; "It might have been!"

Hell is the final penalty of sin. Hell does not mean cessation of existence. The New Testament writers expanded on Jesus' words "kill the soul" with the expression "second death" (Rev. 20:6, 14). When a person opens his life to God, he receives life, which never ends. Hell is the second death where the blessings and fellowship of God never come to a person.

C. S. Lewis wrote of the second death in his book entitled *The Great Divorce,* a fantasy about heaven and hell. Lewis imaginatively pictures hell as a gloomy city drenched by a perpetual cold rain. As his story of hell opens, the streets are deserted except for a line of people waiting for a bus to take them to heaven. No matter how many board, the bus never fills. Those who arrive in heaven, don't like it and take the next bus back.

Though presented rather fancifully, Lewis depicts the reality of the second death. He describes the people's existences as they move farther and farther away from the bus depot. They become more involved with hell than with wanting to go to heaven. All of the characters are dead, but some are deader than others. There is no exercise of the will in their lives. They are in anguish but they refuse God's invitation to "Come." They are shut up with themselves, which is part of what Lewis described as the great divorce from God.

People in hell are successful rebels to the end. They have refused the Lord. The Lord will not intrude in anyone's life on earth to help solve the inward conflicts, to give meaning to life, or to grant life. The doors of hell seem to be locked from the inside. To be sure, no one in hell wishes to remain. They loathe the place, disliking themselves, but they never take the first step to self-abandonment. They want to leave, but they do not will to leave. They are locked in with a selfish soul. Unsaved people spend eternity filled with their unresolved anger, greed, jealousy, and lust.

SOCIAL ANIMOSITY

Hell means to be deprived of meaningful relationships with
people. To be locked in hell away from others with our own
selfishness seems anguish enough. But hell is a place where
other selfish people are, striving to relate to each other. The
discord of interpersonal entanglements makes the torment
of hell even worse. If we really want a glimpse of hell, we
should look at the suspicion, disdain, envy, rivalry, jealousy,
ill-will, and hatred of persons toward one another here on
earth. Hell is filled with people like that, who care for no one
but themselves.

Sin disrupts personal relationships. God created man with
the need for human companionship and friendship. God
made Eve because it was "not good that the man should be
alone" (Gen. 2:18). Everyone needs acceptance, love,
understanding, and friendship from other people, and every
person needs to give acceptance, love, understanding, and
friendship to other people. The good life on earth depends on
harmony among us. But our relationships with other
people suffer because we are selfish. The story of Adam in
the Garden of Eden might be the story of the first man,
but it clearly tells us what all of us are like. Each of us desires
to run life according to our selfish desires. We do not want
to submit to God's will. God meant for man to put God
in first place, and to love our neighbors as ourselves. Jesus
gave God's command in the words: "Thou shalt love the
Lord thy God with all thy heart, and with all thy soul, and
with all thy mind. This is the first and great commandment.
And the second is like unto it, Thou shalt love thy neighbour
as thyself. On these two commandments hang all the law
and the prophets" (Matt. 22:37-40). Man reversed God's
order by putting himself first. As a result, God and other
people become a threat. All sin, therefore, is a challenge to
God's rule over us.

Sin became a social problem when Cain, out of the hatred
of his brother, because of his own selfish desires, murdered
him. This episode in Genesis gives in microcosm a picture
of all of us. Sin reveals itself in all of our hostilities against
others. Since the beginning of the human race, man has
had a hard time living with other people because he is selfish.

Selfishness makes it hard to get along with others as all of history shows. Wars, crimes, and violence go on non-stop. Life all about us confirms that envy, malice, ill-will, hatred, and jealousy are a constant problem among us. The world seems to be a jungle whose motto is "survival of the most selfish."

James summed up the cause of all these relations. "From whence come wars and fightings among you? come they not hence, even of your lusts that war in your members? Ye lust, and have not: ye kill, and desire to have, and cannot obtain: ye fight and war, yet ye have not, because ye ask not" (Jas. 4:1, 2). In other words, James said that because people do not submit to God, they have conflicts with others from their selfish desires. Man's self-love, self-trust, and self-assertion cause social unrest.

If our world survives, human relationships must be strengthened. World leaders talk about the need for people of all kinds to live and work together in the same world. Government seeks to make laws to help people live together in peace. Psychology has increased its study into human nature seeking to find out what causes us to act or react. The cure for poor relationships lies in dealing with the cause, namely self-centeredness. To remove conflicts, selfishness must be replaced with selflessness. None of us can work it within ourselves. Only God can help us to put him first and to love our neighbors as ourselves.

On the basis of getting right with Jesus, one begins the journey of loving his neighbor as himself. God provides the means of living together by a common fellowship with Jesus Christ. But the unsaved will not give up their selfishness. The selfish person seeks his own desires at the expense of others, which breeds more and more divisions. Life on earth becomes a hell of selfish confrontation.

Samuel Becket's play *Waiting for Godot* points out the tension between ungodly people. Two characters, Estagon and Vladimir, cannot stand each other, yet they cannot stand to be apart from each other. Only by keeping up the illusion that they are waiting for someone to change things can they live with each other.

Death does not seem to change personal relations. It

intensifies them. Think briefly for a moment about the
relations of saved people. They give up being selfish and
depend upon the Savior. They love God, trust him, and
obey his will. In this earthly life they think of fellow
Christians as "brothers in Christ" or "fellow citizens" of
the kingdom of God. They try to think of other people as
God thinks. The saved are not exempt completely from
conflicts with each other in their earthly life. But their lives
beyond will be complete harmony with God and with their
fellowman. Death perfects the relationships that are being
perfected on earth. There will be no interpersonal conflicts
in heaven.

Now think about the future of unsaved people. During
their earthly life, they would not give up their selfishness.
Hence, their life beyond intensifies their self-will, self-trust,
and self-assertion. C. S. Lewis in *The Great Divorce* pictured
hell as "the grey town" where people lived who quarrel
and bicker all the time. They have lost the meaning of
genuine relationships with other people. They move farther
and farther from meaning something to one another.

No words could fully describe the social animosity which
death brings to the unsaved. To think of the worst discord
on earth is to get but a small picture of an eternity shut up
with selfish people. Hell means to be deprived of people
who can mean something to other people. One can never
know meaningful relationships in hell. Each person there
loves only himself. The phrase "misery loves company"
is revised in hell to "misery hates company." In hell people
contest others' desires and hinder themselves. Sinners
cast themselves off from others. Those in hell are both
without and against people. The country priest in Bernanos'
novel *The Diary of a Country Priest* exclaimed, "Hell
is—not to love any more, . . . Madame. . . . The sorrow, the
unutterable sorrow of these charred stones which once were
men, is that they have nothing more to be shared."[3]

A portion of hell's suffering must be the separation from
good people. In the parable of the marriage feast, Jesus
taught that the future life for the wicked meant being
deprived of the joys of the feast. The host of the marriage
feast ordered those who refused to prepare for the wedding to

be put out of the festivities. Part of the torment of these people was to see and to hear the joy of the guests at the wedding feast but not be able to take part.

In addition to being set apart from good people, hell is a place where people are locked in with those who refused God. Some refused the Lord stronger than others and rebelled more openly. Jesus said of them: "Then shall he [God] say also unto them on the left hand, Depart from me, ye cursed, into everlasting fire, prepared for the devil and his angels" (Matt. 25:41). The author of Revelation described the inhabitants of hell, "For without are dogs, and sorcerers, and whoremongers, and murderers, and idolators, and whosoever loveth and maketh a lie" (Rev. 22:15). This makes hell a bad place filled with people who can't get along with each other.

We think sometimes that we would like to be isolated on a lonely island in the South Pacific. But on one side of our nature is the need for human companionship. We shiver at the thought of being isolated forever with only ourselves. We need friends to share life with us. We need to love and to be loved. We desire understanding and to be understood. We want to help others and to be helped by them. But to think of life without other people means hell. Saint Theresa of Avila once said, "Hell is the place where no one loves." Why people do not love is evident. They are so wrapped up in themselves that they will not seek the interest of any other person.

Hell also means an absence of love from others. Everyone not only needs to love, but they need to be loved. Everyone in hell is too selfish to love, so no one receives love. No one in hell ever gets a letter of appreciation, a compliment from another person, a kind word, an expression of kindness, a loving touch, or any other expression of care.

There is a fable about a man visiting heaven and afterwards visiting hell. In hell the visitor saw a strange sight. People were locked together at their elbows. They could not pull themselves apart. Yet, they pulled and jerked trying to get apart. They quarreled and complained. Then the visitor went to heaven. Surprisingly, he saw people living locked together just like the people in hell. But in heaven each person helped others and fed each other. God directs his people to love and care for others, and to seek the highest good of other people, but the unsaved think only of themselves. They are known by their envy, quarrels, malice, jealousy, hatred, hostility, and ill-will.

SEPARATION FROM GOD

The most dreadful thing about hell is that people are separated from God. Being apart from God's presence forever would mean to miss God's highest purpose and goal of life and to deprive oneself of the greatest relationship one could experience. Those who are in hell are people who have chosen to manage life without God. The next life will not change their desire to rebel against God.

One of the saddest statements of our Lord was spoken in the parable of the sheep and goats. To the unrighteous people on his left hand he said, "Depart from me, ye cursed, into everlasting fire, prepared for the devil and his angels" (Matt. 25:41). Two words in this statement present the awesome terror of hell. "Depart" depicts a sentence of doom. It describes a going away from someone. Perhaps the best way to describe the scene is the sorrow of seeing a loved one go away in death. The pronoun me represents a departure from God. No sadder experience can be conceived than the sentence to leave the presence of God. Yet, Jesus taught that if we are not willing to open our lives to the Lord, it will close the opportunity for God to dwell in us and to bring his blessings.

Sin separates us from God. After Adam and Eve sinned, they hid themselves from God (Gen. 3:8). Sin blinds the eyes of men so that they think of God as an enemy to be avoided. Isaiah said it was sin that separated Judah from God, "Behold, the Lord's hand is not shortened, that is cannot save; neither his ear heavy, that it cannot hear: but your iniquities have separated between you and your God, and your sins have hid his face from you, that he will not hear" (Isa. 59:1, 2). During Isaiah's time, God's people blamed God for their problems. They considered God as their enemy rather than their friend. They thought God delayed their return to Palestine. Isaiah diagnosed the cause of their feeling about God—their own sins.

Paul often wrote about sin separating a person from God, and the unsaved as being "separated from Christ," "far off," "without God in the world."

To live apart from God is to be apart from his fellowship and blessings. God doesn't leave us—we leave him. Intimacy with God was pictured in the life of Enoch. "And Enoch walked with God: and he was not; for God took him" (Gen. 5:24). Enoch represents those who trust and obey. But to the contrary there are those who disbelieve and disobey and walk further from the Lord. Finally, they go so far that they are separated from him forever. Hell is not a place where people have been abandoned by God or where God has ceased to love people. God continues to love, but he will not force anyone to trust him.

One can choose to be known as a child of God or to remain an alien. In the parable of the wheat and tares (Matt. 13:24-30, 35-43) Jesus taught that the righteous and the unrighteous live together on earth, but their natures are not alike. The harvest in the parable speaks of the final setting apart of the saved from the unsaved. Those who are reckoned as wheat reign in intimate fellowship with the Lord forever. The tares in the story are the unrighteous, who will dwell forever in torment away from the blessings and fellowship of the Lord.

Jesus taught that on the judgment day God will separate the righteous from the unrighteous. This fact can be seen in the parable of the sheep and the goats (Matt. 25:31-46). The picture of a shepherd separating the sheep from the goats at the end of the day was a common sight in Jesus' day. At the end of the age, God will in the same way separate the unrighteous from the righteous.

Not even the Bible attempts to depict the terror of being separated from God. The language telling about it has the sound of a door going shut forever. The minor frustration of losing car keys or house keys cannot be compared to the misery and torment of locking yourself away from God forever.

Final separation from God means to experience God's

wrath forever. Often we neglect the biblical teaching on
God's wrath. "For our God is a consuming fire" (Heb. 12:29).
"For the wrath of God is revealed from heaven against
all ungodliness and unrighteousness of men" (Rom. 1:18).
The term *wrath of God* does not mean revenge. It is not
something which God turns "on" or "off" depending upon his
mood. God's wrath cannot be compared to a temper
tantrum. The term *wrath of God* describes the reverse side
of God's love. God governs the universe based on moral
laws which he has given. He said that those who rebel against
him will receive his wrath. Wrath is God's attitude against
sins. God built into life a process of moral cause and effect.
Spurning what God has said cuts the rebel off from the
presence and blessings of the Lord. Paul said that they "shall
be punished with everlasting destruction from the presence
of the Lord, and from the glory of his power" (2 Thes. 1:9).

Final separation from God must be seen as the Bible
describes it. Often people ask, "How can a person be finally
separated from God? Doesn't God live everywhere?" It is true
that God is everywhere (Psa. 139:7-12). Yet, God does not
always appear in love. Hell is made even more terrible
by the fact that God is there, but he is present in wrath.
Heaven seems to be wonderful because God is present in all
his love. From this atmosphere of love the wicked have
chosen to rebel. Therefore, no one can say that a cruel God
abandons people in hell.

Eternal separation is pictured as spiritual death, the worst
penalty of sin. Death means separation of the soul from
God. Spiritual death or "second death" mentioned frequently
in the New Testament means absence of God within this
life. Eternal death is the soul's permanent separation from
God resulting from willful and final disobedience.

Learning what Jesus and the other divinely inspired writers
meant by their unique language requires careful study. The
more I think about the Bible's truths about hell, the more
the figure of the isolation ward seems to fit the biblical
description. Try, if you can, to grasp the tragedy of a person
being eternally in isolation, separated from God. The very
thought of hell should cause one to choose life with Christ.

FIVE
THE INSTANT REPLAY

When some people think about hell, they turn immediately to Jesus' story of the rich man and Lazarus (Luke 16:19-31). Some seem to think that Jesus told the story to satisfy curiosities about heaven and hell. The story teaches us about the life beyond, but this was not the full thrust of the parable. Jesus told the story to teach about the seriousness of life as seen by two different types of people.

The parable shows that we can live for the Lord by loving him and by loving our neighbor as ourselves. To choose the Lord means the joy of serving him on earth and the joy that will be ours in the life beyond. But we can also shut the Lord out of our lives, be obsessed with material things, and be robbed of life's true happiness, suffering torment and anguish in the next life as a result.

Jesus told the story in two scenes. The first scene takes place on earth, showing a rich man and a beggar, and how each lived on earth. The rich man lived in ease and luxury, dressed in purple and fine linen, in a palatial home. He "fared sumptuously" each day.

The beggar, Lazarus, lived outside the gates of the rich man's dwelling, where he ate the scraps from the rich man's table. His body was covered with sores which the dogs licked. Evidently he had no strength to drive them off.

The second scene takes place after the death of both men.

Lazarus was "carried by the angels to Abraham's bosom," an expression which means that the beggar entered the fellowship with God and his people. Instead of misery, the beggar enjoyed eternal bliss and intimate fellowship, feasting at the heavenly banquet.

The rich man went to Hades, corresponding to the Sheol of the Old Testament. The word *hades* seems to be equivalent to *gehenna*, the place of torment. In his agony, he cried for Lazarus to do something for him. He was alive, awake, and suffering, not in soul sleep as some believe about the afterlife. The rich man's thirst and torment in flames were real, showing the terrible reality of hell. More tragic than anything was the fact that the rich man was separated from God. He saw the blessings of God and the intimacy of fellowship with God of which he could never be a part. The rich man's desires could never be satisfied. His request for Lazarus' help could not be granted.

What seems to be the sin that sent the rich man to hell? Did he get his money dishonestly? The story does not say. He passed Lazarus daily, but he felt no compassion. He thought too much of himself. Being rich or being dishonest were not his crimes. His sin was the love of himself.

Behind Jesus' language there are truths which apply to life on earth and the life beyond. Self-consciousness remained both for the rich man and Lazarus. They were dead, but they were vividly conscious beyond the grave. Identity remained. Death did not destroy their personalities. The rich man remained his selfish self. Lazarus was still the man who allowed God to help him.

One clear fact from this story is that death does not destroy memory. When the rich man sought relief from his anguish in hell, Abraham said, "Son, remember . . ." Abraham invited him to reflect on his past. He wanted him to go through the scenes of his selfishness. The rich man remembered that in his earthly life he lived for himself. Then he remembered his five brothers and the memory caused deep anguish and torment.

A part of hell's torment will be the perpetual recall of previous life on earth. Instant replay is a clever addition to television. When we watch football games or other

events, we can see the exciting plays again. The camera can
also give close-ups and different angles of the play. Spectators
enjoy the instant replay, but it could be painful at times
for the players to see again their blunders. In hell one looks
back and sees the scenes of life over again, which for
some will surely be one of the most severe punishments.

THE REJECTED CHRIST

Abraham, in effect, says to every condemned person in hell,
"Son, remember..." One prominent remembrance will be
the life and ministry of Jesus Christ. His coming is the event
in history on which every life will be judged. Jesus brought
meaning and purpose to life. Christianity is not rules or laws
but a relationship to the person of Christ. Attempts to treat
his coming as myth have failed. History records his coming
to the land of Palestine. He lived in Nazareth, ministered
throughout Palestine, and died in Jerusalem. He arose
from the grave and ministered for forty more days. Then he
ascended into heaven with the promise of a victorious return.

Jesus has a vital place in history. He gives meaning
to life, meaningful relationships to others, and makes
possible our relationship with God. If one opens his life to
Christ, he attains the ultimate in life. But if one refuses
Christ, he will be forced to live with his choice throughout
eternity. In the next life, he will painfully remember Jesus
Christ, which will add immeasurable suffering to the torment
of hell.

Abraham continuously calls upon the people in hell to
remember who Jesus Christ is. "Son, remember..." They
remember that Jesus is more than those the world calls
great people. They will recall that he is not just one of the
many heroes of history. He is Jesus Christ, the Son of
God. Every person in hell will inevitably remember Jesus
Christ, and that he really is who he claimed to be, the Son
of God.

Seeing who Jesus is reminds us that rejecting him is no
small matter. Rejecting Jesus is not just refusing a great
teacher. It is refusing to allow the one, true, only God to
be the sovereign Lord of life. The glaring reality of who

Jesus is will be a theme replayed in hell constantly.

Abraham perpetually reminds the people in hell to remember what Jesus Christ did. "Son, remember..." In Jesus' visit to earth he did something for every man that man could not do for himself. Some think that even those hours Christ spent on the cross will be replayed to those in hell.

Jesus' death on the cross was a sacrifice on behalf of man's sins. The New Testament and especially the book of Hebrews names Jesus as "the Great High Priest" and the final sacrifice for sin. The shed blood on the cross dramatically emphasizes what Christ did for sinful man and the high cost he was willing to pay.

Jesus' death has to be a focal point of history. It allowed a broken, fractured world the possibility of being reconciled. One of the horrible memories of hell has to be what Jesus did for mankind through his death and resurrection. In hell the barrier remains between God and the unsaved. Painful will be the memory that what Jesus did on Calvary solved every spiritual problem which man had with God. Because of who Jesus is and what he has done, abundant blessings could have come.

Think for a moment what Jesus could have meant to those in hell. He could have forgiven their sins. He could have declared them right with God. He could have removed the barrier of sin standing in the way of their reconciliation and their freedom. But Jesus would not forgive unless there was expressed repentance, faith, and confession. No matter how guilty the sinners were, they need not to have gone to hell. Jesus could have restored them to a right relationship with God if they had allowed him.

Jesus could have given a new life to every person who has gone to hell. They sought various other means to find the ultimate purpose in life, looking for meaning. Jesus came to bring them life, but they refused. Instead, they offered excuses such as: "I would become a Christian, but I can't hold out." "I'm waiting until I am better." "There are too many hypocrites in the church." "I'll wait." All through their lives they thought they had to "do it their way," but they found that doing it themselves brought eternal death.

The replay of how Jesus could have brought newness of life constantly flashes across the screen of hell.

The opposite of eternal joy and blessed fellowship with Jesus is to be in a place where being with Jesus is forfeited forever. In *The Diary of a Country Priest,* Bernanos said, "Just you wait. Wait for the first quarter-of-an-hour's silence. Then the Word will be heard of men—not the voice they rejected, which spoke so quietly: I am the Way, the Resurrection, and the Life—but the voice from the depths: I am the door forever locked, the road which leads nowhere, the life, the everlasting dark!"[1]

THE TORTURED CONSCIENCE

The words of Abraham to the rich man in hell—"Son, remember . . ." show that part of eternal punishment will be the constant guilt feelings about life on earth. The rich man's suffering was his tortured memory about his selfish attitude toward life. When he had an opportunity to think, he remembered his apathetic attitude toward Lazarus. He remembered his brothers when he was in hell, but not on earth.

Alan Richardson said of the conscience: "Every human being who is not clearly imbecile has a knowledge of right and wrong."[2] In the Garden of Eden after Adam and Eve sinned against God, they felt guilty and hid themselves. Time could not erase the guilt Joseph's brothers felt because of their injustice to Joseph. When they reunited in Egypt, they confessed: "We are verily guilty concerning our brother, in that we saw the anguish of his soul, when he besought us, and we would not hear; therefore is this distress come upon us" (Gen. 42:21).

The memory of past mistakes bothers all of us. After his sin of adultery with Bathsheba and his murder of Uriah, David's life was miserable. The memory of God's broken laws paraded endlessly before him, according to his own words: "My sin is ever before me" (Psa. 51:3). His affair with Bathsheba was enjoyable at first, but the memory of having broken God's law was painful. That scene of the woman taking a bath must have replayed perpetually. How many times he must have wished that he had looked the other way.

God gave all of us the ability to know right from wrong. But no one's conscience is infallible, since it can be abused to the point that it no longer responds to truth. But the fact that we can override the conscience does not remove the fact that God put one within each of us.

Someone may ask, "Does death destroy the conscience?" If one believes in annihilation of the soul after death, the answer is yes. But if we accept what the Bible says about hell, we must say no. Both men in the parable kept their identity, their recognition of each other, their minds, and their memories. According to the New Testament, death does not seem to destroy the conscience.

We all sometimes feel the pain of a guilty conscience. No measuring device has yet been produced by psychiatry to measure the pain caused by guilty feelings. Some suffer more pain from a guilty conscience than others, but the truth remains that every violation against God will hurt us. Mark Twain's Huckleberry Finn said the feeling of guilt "takes up more room than all the rest of a person's insides."

William Shakespeare's Lady Macbeth was troubled with "thick coming fancies" regarding her plot to murder the king. Shakespeare said a guilty mind is "full of scorpions." If he had lived in our time, he might have said that Lady Macbeth was troubled with instant replays of her guilty acts. When Macbeth saw the tortures into which sin had plunged his wife, he pled with the court physician.

Cure her of that.
Canst thou not minister to a mind diseased.
Pluck from the memory a rooted sorrow,
Raze out the written troubles of the brain
And with some sweet oblivious antidote
Cleanse the stuff'd bosom of that perilous stuff
Which weighs upon the heart?[3]

Guilt can rob us of physical health. Doctors speak of some patients having physical symptoms caused by feelings of guilt. Guilt can destroy emotional and mental health, causing anxiety, frustration, despair, and even suicide. Guilt destroys fellowship with God.

Another appropriate question might be: "Does death eliminate the pain of a guilty conscience?" Evidently not, since the New Testament teaches that personality remains beyond the grave. Death does not destroy guilt feelings. A poet described the pain of guilt:

The ghosts of forgotten actions
  Come floating before my sight,
And the things that I thought were dead things
  Were alive with a terrible might,
And the vision of all my past life
  Was a dreadful thing to face
Alone, alone with my conscience
  In that strange and fearful place.[4]

Guilt feelings can sometimes be relieved temporarily. Some people try to punish themselves as if that would silence their accusing conscience. Others justify their actions by rationalizing away the guilt. Some blame their sins on other people. Others seek to compensate for it by some pious deeds. All of these might give temporary relief for a guilty conscience.

The New Testament, however, teaches that there is only one way to relieve a guilty conscience, the way offered in the Christian gospel. Jesus can cure the hurt caused by sin only one way—by removing the guilt.

Hell has to be a terrible place because no guilt is ever relieved or forgiven there. Not even temporary relief is found there. The rich man cried for mercy, begging for Lazarus to help him. The message of this story is that there is no relief for a burning tongue or a tortured conscience.

A FATEFUL CHOICE

Abraham's words, "Son, remember," struck sharply within the soul of the rich man. Perhaps he remembered the questions he asked himself: "Should I help this poor beggar? or should I ignore him?" But each time he had ignored him and refused to help was replayed in hell.

Having the ability to make choices sets man apart from the rest of God's creation. Only man can pursue a course of action and choose a destiny. Edwin Markham wrote:

When, in the dim beginning of the years,
God mixed in man the raptures and the tears,
And scattered through his brain the starry stuff,
He said, "Behold! yet this is not enough,
For I must test his spirit to make sure
That he can dare the Vision and endure.
I will withdraw My face,
Veil me in shadow for a certain space,
Leaving behind only a broken clue,
A crevice where the glory glimmers through,
Some whisper from the sky,
Some footprint in the road to track Me by.
I will leave man to make the fateful guess,
Will leave him torn between the no and yes,
Leave him unresting till he rests in Me,
Drawn upward by the choice that makes him free—
Leave him in tragic loneliness to choose,
With all in life to win or all to lose."[5]

God could have made man with a predetermined destiny, but man then would have been not unique and distinct, but a mere robot. Many have the idea that the New Testament term *predestination* means that God chooses our destiny, that he selects some people for salvation and some for damnation. The New Testament use of *predestination* in no way destroys the idea of man's will, nor does it imply that God determines man's fate. God gave man the power of choice, and this fact makes every person and most decisions of life extremely important.

God wishes that every person would make the right choice. "The Lord is not slack concerning his promise, as some men count slackness; but is longsuffering to us-ward, not willing that any should perish, but that all should come to repentance" (2 Pet. 3:9). God encourages, woos, persuades, urges. But he will never force a decision upon anyone.

Character is shown in the choices we make. When we open our life to God, he makes us what we ought to be. Therefore, man can become what he ought to become. But, man can also close his life to God and be wrapped up in selfishness.

The rich man's decisions determined his character. His selfishness caused him to live without noticing the needs of a beggar at his gates. William James in his chapter on habit says, "The hell to be endured hereafter, of which theology tells, is no worse than the hell we make for ourselves in this world by habitually fashioning our characters in the wrong way.... As we become permanent drunkards by so many separate drinks, so we become saints in the moral, and authorities and experts in the practical and scientific spheres, by so many separate acts and hours of work."[6]

People choose to rebel. Rebellion produces acts, which produce character, and character becomes permanent. Through a series of choices comes a fixity of character. The memory of these acts furnishes the scenes for the replays of the times where character could have gone in a different direction.

Fisher Humphreys in his book, *Thinking about God*, tells of a televised fiction story in which a bank robber is killed by the police. A man in a white suit, supposedly the robber's guardian angel, raised him from the dead. The angel said, "I am here to give you whatever you want." He took the robber to a large store stocked with beautiful furniture, a well-stocked bar, stereophonic music, and beautiful girls. At first the robber enjoyed it, but soon he became bored. Then the robber wanted to go to the pool hall. With his first shot, he sank every ball on the table. Soon he became bored with this too. He told the angel that he wanted to rob a bank. The angel arranged it, and the robbery progressed smoothly. The robber escaped with large bags of money. He repeated the act of robbery several times. Soon this bored him. Then the angel asked him what he wanted. The robber could not think of anything. The story closed with a dramatic dialogue:

"Well, Angel, I'd better tell you something. You see, there's been a mistake. On earth I was a bad guy, see? So I really belong in hell with the other bad guys. I mean I don't really desire to be here in heaven, you understand. So send me away from heaven."

The angel replied, "My friend, you have made a mistake. Whatever made you think this is heaven?"[7]

If we insist on having our own way, we are certain to create a hell for ourselves. Paul repeated the statement "God gave them up" three times in the first chapter of Romans (vv. 24, 26, 28). Whether we choose God or not is a choice which each of us must make.

God encouraged Adam and Eve to eat of all trees in the garden but he warned them against eating from one tree. Their decision determined their destiny, resulting in death and separation from God. Paul traced man's depravity to man's own choice. The people sought to live without God, and the Lord granted them their wish.

Many people today show no interest in knowing and loving God or each other. God will allow such people to spend eternity continuing to choose a life apart from him. He has persuaded them through his messengers, spoken positively through varied experiences, and moved them by his Spirit. But he will not force anyone to live with him.

Psychiatry teaches us that every one of our experiences are stored somewhere in the memory. The recall might be difficult, but nonetheless, the actions and the attitudes lie somewhere in the memory banks of our minds. Death does not destroy them. Those without Christ will someday undergo the suffering of having the memory of a life without God replayed perpetually. And the experience of it is what hell is all about.

SIX
THINK GOOD ABOUT GOD

Any investigation into the doctrine of hell prompts many
serious questions about the goodness of God. The Bible
teaches both the goodness of God and the eternal separation
in hell, and trying to reconcile these two truths presents
a difficult problem. Upon investigating the horrible condition
of hell, the questions arise: "How can a good God allow
such a place as hell to exist?" and "Doesn't hell contradict
God's love?" or "How can a good God torment people
endlessly?" A careful study of the doctrine of God is needed
as one studies the doctrine of hell.

Much of what the Bible says about hell is in Jesus' own
words. Jesus' expression "unquenchable fire," "undying
worms," and "weeping and gnashing of teeth" teach the
horrible fate of the wicked. Other New Testament writers
supported Jesus' ideas about punishment for the wicked after
death.

But, on the other hand, the Bible says much about love,
grace, and the goodness of God, especially in Jesus' life and
ministry.

Serious Bible students through the years have wrestled
with trying to reconcile the goodness of God with eternal
punishment. John Stuart Mill, a nineteenth-century British
philosopher, popularized some ideas on the dilemma of
God's goodness and endless torment. He reasoned that it was
not within the nature of a good person to torment another

person endlessly. One might punish another severely for a
while but not continuously. Mill concluded that a good God
could not punish sinners forever. Using this line of reasoning,
he and others have rejected hell, claiming that it violates
God's goodness.

The Bible teaches both the reality of hell and the goodness
of God. To deny either of these truths is to depart from
the teaching of God's Word. Search the Scriptures from
Genesis to Revelation and discover the truth that God's love
is like an eagle's care for her young: "As an eagle stirreth
up her nest, fluttereth over her young, spreadeth abroad her
wings, taketh them, beareth them on her wings" (Deut. 32:11).
Psalm 103:13 says, "Like as a father pitieth his children,
so the Lord pitieth them that fear him." Speaking through
the prophet Jeremiah, God said "I have loved thee with an
everlasting love" (Jer. 31:3). From the New Testament come
the words: "For God so loved the world . . ." (John 3:16).
Without a question, we believe the Bible teaches God's love
and goodness.

We must look at both the fact of God's love and God's wrath.
These truths must be balanced. No Bible doctrine could
distort the picture of God more than hell. Overemphasizing
either God's holiness or God's love could lead to two
prominent distortions of God.

Stressing God's love to the neglect of his holiness presents
the picture that God is a sentimental grandfather. Our boys
love to visit their grandparents because they are able to get
away with behavior we won't allow at home. But the Bible
presents God, not as a tolerating, gentle grandfather, but as a
loving, kind father. Reading sentimentality into God's
character misses what the Bible says about God's stern
judgment.

On the other extreme, some have presented God as a tyrant
who enjoys seeing the wicked suffer; as a stern judge,
anxiously waiting to give every person what he deserves. The
Bible's picture of God has the correct balance. Jesus showed
the Father to be one who knows, cares, and gives help to
his creatures. He is described as being like a shepherd, looking
for his lost sheep. He is like a father who waits the return
of prodigal children. The depth of God's love for humanity

is seen when he went to the cross. Jesus revealed the Father to be one who loves.

But Jesus also denounced human wickedness. He preached on *gehenna*. Jesus clearly revealed what God has always been and what he will always be. Jesus presented God perfectly with a balance between God's love and God's holiness that explains his severity on sin.

The more we know about God and his holiness the more we understand the reality and necessity of hell, and the less are our resentments and questions about God's goodness.

TRUE TO HIS CHARACTER

Let us look closely into what the Bible says about God. One facet of God's nature is that he never speaks, thinks, or acts contrary to his character. At one time Abraham wrestled with the dilemma of God's love and God's judgment on sin. Being aware of impending destruction of the cities of Sodom and Gomorrah, Abraham asked, "Wilt thou also destroy the righteous with the wicked?" (Gen. 18:23). The destruction of people in these cities disturbed him greatly. Yet, he knew their wickedness. After an intense inward struggle, he said, "Shall not the Judge of all the earth do right?" (Gen. 18:25).

Abraham then reasoned that the cities should not be destroyed for the sake of fifty righteous persons. The Lord agreed. Abraham then wondered if he could find fifty righteous people, so he pleaded successively for the salvation of the city with forty-five, forty, thirty, twenty, and then ten righteous persons. In each case, the Lord agreed to spare the city. But evidently they could not find even ten. God then acted in judgment, in accordance with his character.

The Bible states explicitly several facets about God's moral character. It speaks of God's holiness. The term *holiness* describes the moral excellence of God, his moral perfection. He is good in the absolute sense of the word. His holiness is foundational for his righteousness and love.

Learning then that God is holy, we reasonably conclude that God repudiates all forms of evil. Augustus H. Strong said that "holiness is self-affirming purity."[1] God could not be described

as holy if he permitted evil as a part of his will. All through
the Bible God always acted in accordance with his holiness.
When the children of Israel crossed the Red Sea, they said,
"Who is like unto thee, O Lord, among the gods? Who is like
thee, glorious in holiness, fearful in praises, doing wonders?"
(Exod. 15:11). Frequently God acted in judgment on the
people of Israel. In doing so he was being true to his character
of holiness.

God could not have been described as the "holy one of
Israel" if he tolerated idolatry, rebellion, and human injustices
against others. He destroyed the world in a flood. He rained
fire and brimstone on Sodom and Gomorrah because he is
holy.

God's holiness made hell necessary. God said, "Be ye holy,
for I am holy." God never compromises his holy being to
moral evil. To say that God is holy means that he does what
ought to be done. Hell, then, is God's persistent opposition to
sin. As long as man continues to sin, hell will continue
to exist.

The Bible teaches that God is righteous, which means that
God is free from all defect and taint of character. It means
moral purity and absolute freedom of stain and guilt. The
Bible, speaking of the righteousness of God, says: "This then is
the message which we have heard of him and declare unto
you, that God is light, and in him is no darkness at all"
(1 John 1:5). James described God as one in whom there is "no
variableness, neither shadow of turning" (Jas. 1:17). Jesus
prayed, "O righteous Father" (John 17:25). When the Bible
speaks of the righteousness of God, it means the self-
affirmation of God in favor of the right and in opposition to
the wrong.

God's righteousness helps us to understand the reasons for
hell. God uses diverse means to reveal his moral requirements
—conscience of men, law and prophets, teachings of Christ,
and the character of Jesus. When men lack righteousness, God
must condemn to be true to his character. He must punish
transgressors. Scholars call this facet of God's action "punitive
righteousness." To overlook or to neglect sin would be to
act contrary to his nature. Hell does not mean that God does
not love people—it means that he hates sin.

To understand why God must punish sin we must look at Jesus' life and ministry. Jesus loved sinners and yearned to help them. Each time a person showed sorrow for sin Jesus forgave him or her. To an extremely sinful woman Jesus said, "Thy sins are forgiven" (Luke 7:48). Yet, those who persisted in unbelief, Jesus condemned. He called the unrepentant "hypocrites," "sons of hell," and the "offspring of vipers." God condemns only those who will not repent. Hell or the consequences of sin cannot be blamed on God.

God is good and always does what is right. If we believe that God is holy and righteous, then we must believe that hell is part of his will.

Ask yourself, "Would God be holy if he did not stand against evil?" Ask yourself again, "Would God be righteous if he did not condemn unrighteousness?" It seems clear then that hell does not contradict God's character or cast a shadow on his goodness.

TENDER IN HIS CONCERN

The Bible shows that God is extremely tender in his concern for people, as seen, for example, in the story of Abraham pleading for the wicked cities of Sodom and Gomorrah. One could easily distort the story by presenting only one part of the narrative. "Then the Lord rained upon Sodom and Gomorrah brimstone and fire from the Lord out of heaven; and he overthrew those cities, and all the plain, and all the inhabitants of the cities, and that which grew upon the ground" (Gen. 19:24, 25). To emphasize only judgment neglects God's concern. We see that God greatly desired to spare these cities rather than to destroy them. He pled earnestly and warned fervently before he responded in judgment.

We tend to think of God's wrath on these cities more than God's grace. God told Abraham that he would spare the city for fifty righteous persons. Archaeologists estimate that these cities were densely populated, perhaps as many as 75,000 to 100,000 people. God only asked for fifty righteous people, then agreed to only ten. Compared to the total population, this was a demonstration of God's grace. This story provides

a microcosm of how God cares for people. God could have
rightly destroyed the cities without warning, but he didn't.
God always desires the ultimate good of people.

Contemporary man asks, "How does God feel about me?"
Some read the Bible and conclude that God dislikes man and
earnestly desires to send him to hell. Others read the
Scriptures and believe that God loves everyone and will never
permit anything as bad as hell to happen to them. The former
presents God as a raging tyrant while the latter pictures
him as a sentimental grandfather. Both are wrong, because
God is both loving and holy.

Numerous notions exist about God's love. The Bible
describes God's love as a steadfast love. Some seem to think
that God loves us when we obey and gets angry with us when
we disobey. Using episodes from Old Testament history
they picture God as having temper tantrums, such as turning
Lot's wife into a pillar of salt; sending serpents to bite
the disobedient Israelites; causing the ground to swallow
Korah, Dathan, and Abiram; sending fire from heaven to wipe
out the Assyrians; sending a bear to tear forty people
apart; and numerous other episodes. But if one reads the Old
Testament carefully he will see that from Genesis through
Malachi, God sought man's highest good. When man rebelled
in the garden, he sought for them. When the Israelites
disobeyed and complained in the wilderness, God suffered
extensively with them. God pleaded with them through the
prophets. Reading isolated incidents of vengeance does not
give the complete picture of God.

The Old Testament psalmist pictures God as caring for
people with a steadfast and gracious love. "All the paths of
the Lord are mercy and truth unto such as keep his covenant
and his testimonies" (Psa. 25:10). "Also unto thee, O Lord,
belongeth mercy" (Psa. 62:12).

The choice illustration of God's steadfast love comes from
Hosea's experiences. Gomer, the prophet's wife, left him for
another lover, yet he continued to love Gomer. Hosea's
experience shows us how God feels about people: "When
Israel was a child, then I loved him" (Hos. 11:1).

Paul described God's love: "All day long I have stretched
forth my hands unto a disobedient and gainsaying people"

(Rom. 10:21). Persistently God offered invitations and opportunities, but Israel continued to disobey. Yet God never withheld his love.

Jesus gave dramatic visibility to God's love. One cannot read of his life and ministry without knowing that God cares for people. The finest and fullest expression of God's love was shown when Jesus came to earth to identify with sinful humanity and to give his life on a cross.

Questions arise about God's love from the use of such biblical phrases as "the wrath of God" and the "anger of the Lord." Such expressions confirm that God created an orderly, moral, predictable world with predictable consequences. We know the laws of gravity, that if we jump off a high building, we fall to the ground. Likewise, God structured the world on moral maxims. Therefore, the "wrath of God" means that the principles by which God ordered the universe have been violated, and not that God has capriciously punished a person.

The biblical writers conceived of God's love as being like a father's. "Wherefore David blessed the Lord before all the congregation: and David said, Blessed be thou, Lord God of Israel our father, for ever and ever" (1 Chron. 29:10). Jesus said, "After this manner therefore pray ye: Our Father" (Matt. 6:9). One should not equate fathers with softness or sentimentality. A good father won't allow his child to act as he pleases. There is something wrong with paternal love which makes no demands or warns of no consequences. In the same manner, no one could respect a God who allows us to do anything we please.

It is also true that a good father is not a tyrant. There is something wrong with parental love which constantly demands submission to a selfish parental desire.

Good earthly fathers balance love and judgment. God deserves the name *Father* in the absolute sense of the word. God always does that which is right. He is both lenient and disciplinary at the same time, like a longsuffering father. "The Lord is not slack concerning his promise, as some men count slackness; but is longsuffering to us-ward, not willing that any should perish, but that all should come to repentance" (2 Pet. 3:9). But God also disciplines, and when he does, it is for his children's betterment, and not a capricious outburst of anger.

The insights on God's love furnish some basic truth about hell. God demands obedience from us because he seeks our highest good. He loves too much to be content with anything but the best. The punishment of hell does not reflect an unkind God who does not care, but disobedient people who were unresponsive to God's desire for the best for their lives.

TRUSTED WITH CHOICES

From the Bible we learn that God trusts people with the power of choice. God gives every person the chance either to walk with him or to walk away from him. Walking with him actualizes potentials. Walking away from God robs us of what God intended for us to have. God forces no one to go in either direction.

Our actions, to choose or to reject, are influenced by many factors, such as heredity and environment. Though these factors influence our decisions, we cannot call it determinism or fatalism because we do have the gift of self-determination. All of us are blessed and even haunted by our freedom.

Though God be good and free be heaven,
  Not force divine can love compel;
And though the song of sins forgiven
  Might sound through lowest hell,
The sweet persuasion of his voice
  Respects the sanctity of will.
He giveth day: thou hast thy choice
  To walk in darkness still.[2]

As far as we can understand the mystery of God's nature, he did not *have* to bestow freedom to man. But God evidently did not want to play with robots. He created people, who could choose to relate to him in love. He knew that man could respond either in obedience or disobedience. If there ever comes a time when God no longer allows freedom, we will cease to be human. G. K. Chesterton wrote, "Hell is

God's greatest compliment to the reality of human freedom
and the dignity of human personality."[3]

One of the clearest pictures of freedom is found in Jesus'
story of the man who had two sons. The younger boy wanted
to go to the far country. The father knew about the place
and even knew about how the experience could rob him of
life's joys. Yet, the father knew that he could not hinder him.
He allowed the boy to make a bad choice. Evidently the
father did not beg the boy to stay. Because the father
respected him, he gave him the freedom to go. This is exactly
what happens when God gives us choices. Our heavenly
Father grants everyone the opportunity to turn from him.

God gives us the freedom to choose right or wrong, blessing
or destruction. Paul expressed God's response to man's
rebellion in Romans 1:24, 26 by the expression, "God gave
them up." God gave man the privilege of following another
god (v. 24). God permitted man to corrupt life (v. 26). God
allowed men the privilege not to think about God and "gave
them over to a reprobate mind" (v. 28). In each case God
gave people over to the life-style they wanted. Freedom
became the occasion for evil even though a better choice
could have been made.

We have seen that freedom can make a hell on earth. We
can also make the life beyond a heaven or hell. God will allow
people to go to hell if they choose, even though it was
never intended for men. To the unrighteous Jesus said,
"Depart from me, ye cursed, into the everlasting fire,
prepared for the devil and his angels" (Matt. 25:41).
Nikolai Berdyaev says, "Man has a moral right to hell—the
right freely to prefer hell to heaven."[4]

Studying God's gift of choice helps us to understand God's
goodness in reference to hell. God would be a tyrant if he
forced us to be good. Hell should not conjure up bad images of
God, for it proves that God grants us the right to make
our own choices. Harold O. J. Brown called hell "the enduring
monument to the freedom of the human will."[5]

Hell does not result from God's anger. It exists because of
man's choice. C. S. Lewis described two kinds of people.
The first group are those who say to God, "Your will be

done." To the second group who reject him, God says, "Your will be done."

In Saint Paul's Cathedral in London, there hangs an impressive and striking picture by Holman Hunt called *Light of the World*. It shows Jesus standing at a door with a lantern in his hand. Someone once told the artist that he left off the latch for the door. The artist replied, "The handle is inside."

There is no gross contradiction in God's goodness and eternal punishment. God would not be true to his character if he tolerated sin. Yet there is no Scripture that shows God taking delight in tormenting sinners. Because he loves us, he gives us the right either to walk with him or to walk away from him.

SEVEN
BAD WORDS WITH MORE THAN FOUR LETTERS

The Bible has various metaphorical figures to depict the essential *nature* of hell. Various figures such as Valley of Hinnom *(gehenna)*, lake of fire, gnawing worm, weeping and gnashing of teeth, darkness, and other such symbols describe various facets about the experiences of hell. These figures give unmistakable glimpses into the hideous realities of a life apart from God. They send such messages as remorse, suffering, misery, torment, sinfulness, and separation from God.

The Bible also portrays the essential *character* of hell with profound words. An old expression is, "One picture is worth a thousand words." One Hebrew or Greek word often brings numerous pictures to mind.

The images, symbolism, and experiences of life behind the Greek and Hebrew words make the Bible come alive. To know something about the essential characteristics of hell, we must identify and study closely such biblical words as *condemnation, perish, punishment, shall not be forgiven, second death,* and *destruction.* These words communicate some sobering realities about what kind of place hell is. Today we hear all kinds of bad, vulgar words. But perhaps the worst words of human language are those which describe hell; an existence apart from God.

CONDEMNATION

Four Hebrew and Greek words are translated *condemn*, *condemned*, or *condemnation*. These words in their noun and verb forms are used over sixty times in the Bible. *Condemnation* originally had two primary meanings. It was used to convey the reality of judgment and final sentence of doom. It also meant a verdict levied against a person by judges in the courts, by the common judgments of people, or by God's verdict. Usually the word *condemnation* referred to God's verdict either temporary or final against man's selfish rebellion.

Looking in Deuteronomy 25:1 the word *condemnation* was used to describe a judge's verdict. In settling a dispute, the judge will "justify the righteous, and condemn the wicked." He gives a verdict in favor of the person who is in the right and against the person who is in the wrong. But the word has a much more serious meaning. In Isaiah 50:8 the scene is a judgment of world affairs where God vindicates the righteous and condemns the unrighteous. In other references the word *condemn* communicates the reality of God's final doom upon those who refused the Lord.

The word *condemnation* gives an insight into hell as it shows the reality of judgment. Each of us must stand before God and be judged based upon our relationship to Christ, reflected through our good or bad works.

God has appointed a day at the end of time when he will judge every person on the basis of one's relationship to Christ. "He that believeth on him is not condemned: but he that believeth not is condemned already, because he hath not believed in the name of the only begotton Son of God" (John 3:18). To the believers, God will pronounce on that day his blessings on those who will live forever with the Lord and his people. But, tragically, God will pronounce condemnation on those who refused to believe. He sentences them to an existence of doom and condemnation.

Modern man seems to treat the idea of judgment as myth, perhaps because the final judgment has been described in terms hard to reconcile with a God who loves us in Christ. But these misconceptions do not change the fact that everyone will be judged by a loving God.

The word *condemnation* was used by Bible writers to describe the nature of a verdict. In most cases it referred to verdicts rendered by judges in courts or verdicts drawn by the common judgments of people. But it also meant God's judgment on evil.

No words can adequately describe the severity of the sentence of condemnation. It means to depart from the blessings and fellowship of God. Speaking of God's plan for the future, Paul described the angels who would come "in flaming fire taking vengeance on them that know not God, and that obey not the gospel of our Lord Jesus Christ: who shall be punished with everlasting destruction from the presence of the Lord, and from the glory of his power" (2 Thes. 1:8, 9). Each phase amplifies the intense torment of hell. Judgment is not subject to blind facts or the fickle activity of an unjust deity. If a man refuses to live according to God's will, he will experience God's vengeance.

Condemnation can also be described by the expression "the wrath of God." "Jesus, which delivered us from the wrath to come" (1 Thes. 1:10). "For which things' sake the wrath of God cometh on the children of disobedience" (Col. 3:6). Throughout the New Testament we see that God has compassion and love toward the sinners but yet an intense anger against sin. God does not want anyone to perish in his sin, yet there will come a time, called "the day of wrath," when God will express final and irrevocable judgment on sinners.

PERISH

Another word, *perish,* describes both the reality and the essential nature of hell. Twelve closely related Hebrew words and eight Greek words have been translated "perish," "destroy," or "lost." The word *perish* appears over 150 times in the King James Version. The Greek word translated "perish" in John 3:16 *(apollumi)* originally had several meanings. It could describe physical destruction. For example, Jesus spoke about the bread which perishes, or bread which wasted away. Also, the disciples on a stormy sea

cried, "Lord, save us; we perish!" Here it meant that the
disciples, unless rescued, would die.

The word *perish* was used also to describe punishment
for sins while on earth. For example, the author of Deuteronomy used the term *perish* to speak of Israel's consequence
for not trusting the Lord to enter the land of Canaan
(Deut. 4:26; 8:19ff.; 11:17). In the New Testament the
rebellious son in Luke 15:17 said, "I perish with hunger," the
consequences of his bad choice.

The word *perish* has another meaning when speaking of the
life of the unbeliever, as it describes the punishment or
suffering in the world to come. Compare the uses in
John 3:16: "For God so loved the world, that he gave his only
begotten Son, that whosoever believeth in him should
not perish, but have everlasting life" and in John 10:28:
"And I give unto them eternal life; and they shall never
perish, neither shall any man pluck them out of my hand."

The word *perish* in many cases spoke only of a physical
destruction. "And if thy right eye offend thee, pluck it out,
and cast it from thee: for it is profitable for thee that
one of thy members should perish, and not that thy whole
body should be cast into hell" (Matt. 5:29). The same Greek
word was also used in reference to old wineskins. "Neither
do men put new wine into old bottles: else the bottles
break, and the wine runneth out, and the bottles perish"
(Matt. 9:17).

The use of *perish* in John 3:16 refers to the loss of a soul,
showing that hell means not just the loss of a part of life
but the loss of the essence of life. Closely akin to the idea of
perish in John 3:16 are Jesus' words in Matthew 16:26. "For
what is a man profited, if he shall gain the whole world, and
lose his own soul? or what shall a man give in exchange
for his soul?" In this case *perish* doesn't mean extinction or
cessation of life, but as we showed earlier, separation from
God. The soul does not perish like the body. *Perish* is an
awful word, as it denotes the ultimate in evil which can befall
the soul.

One loses his soul by rejecting Christ. Paul said, "For the
preaching of the cross is to them that perish foolishness;

but unto us which are saved it is the power of God" (1 Cor. 1:18). The expressions "that perish" and "are saved" mean respectively, "those in the process of perishing" and "those in the process of being saved." People who are unresponsive to Christ are presently in the process of losing their souls. Hell, therefore, begins with shutting Christ out of life. Life beyond the grave confirms the direction.

The word *perish* describes the inevitable culmination of sin. Hell begins with selfishness. It increases with other expressions of self-interest and self-trust. It ends with the ultimate, inescapable, eternal loss of life.

Hell is where one can see finally what a person is like. Those who live in prejudice exist with intense hatred. Those who live sensually find themselves beset with insatiable passions. As the person dies, so he goes into eternity.

PUNISHMENT

The Bible writers often spoke of punishment for sin. The word *punishment* appears fifty-four times in the Old Testament and eight times in the New Testament of the King James Version. God wanted people to know that he strongly opposed sin. There are three kinds of punishment shown in the Bible. First, we find the idea of retribution, such as the Old Testament referred to as "an eye for an eye and a tooth for a tooth." Second, the word punishment describes God's reaction to sin. The Hebrew verb *paqad* meant "God's judgment against sin." Whenever God came into contact with sin, he opposed it violently. Third, the word punishment describes the consequences of sin. Sin has its inevitable sequel in pain, suffering, and death.

The word *punishment* shows hell to be a real place. In Jesus' parable of a final judgment day, he pictured a final separation, using the symbols of sheep and goats to represent the righteous and unrighteous. To the believers Jesus will say, "Come, ye blessed of my Father, inherit the kingdom prepared for you" (Matt. 25:34). To the unbelievers, the Lord said, "Depart from me, ye cursed, into everlasting fire, prepared for the devil and his angels" (Matt. 25:41).

Commenting on the fate of the unbelievers, he said, "And these shall go away into everlasting punishment: but the righteous into life eternal" (Matt. 25:46). We can see that punishment awaits the unsaved.

It is natural that we should want to know what kind of chastisement the wicked will experience forever. God did not allow the Bible writers to give us full descriptions. Some zealous people have distorted the picture. They describe hell solely on the basis of physical qualities. One artist painted hell as a burning inferno, with demons poking the fire, keeping the flame aglow. Those in hell were shown hanging by their tongues, tormented in the flames, and some being whipped unmercifully. A religious film entitled *The Burning Hell* advertises the nature of punishment to be 20,000 degrees Fahrenheit. Though hell is a terrible place, no such descriptions are mentioned in the Bible.

The nature of eternal punishment is shown many ways. First, the Bible uses metaphorical language to describe spiritual realities. More important than any such phrases as *gehenna*, lake of fire, gnawing worm, is the spiritual truth behind these figures of speech. The most important truth is that hell means a life separated from God. One would have a difficult time trying to make hell any worse, since being separated from God is a far greater punishment than hanging by your tongue, scorching in flames, or taking lashes. Whatever the term *eternal fire* means, it means something as bad and doubtless worse than fire. No earthly image adequately conveys the horrible reality of a life apart from God.

Second, the Bible describes hell's punishment as the absence of any good, which is implied in being separated from God. Apart from him there can be no good. Any type of life apart from God is hell.

Third, the Bible describes punishment as "eternal." The Greek word used was *aionios*. Whatever the exact punishment of hell is, there is no reason to believe that it will cease.

OTHER WORDS

Several other Bible words describe the fate of the unsaved, in fact, some of the worst words that could be spoken. Think of the expression "not forgiven," referring to the lost. Jesus said, "Whosoever speaketh against the Holy Ghost, it shall not be forgiven him, neither in this world, neither in the world to come" (Matt. 12:32). "Not forgiven" is a terrible sentence.

What sin does a person commit that God will not ever forgive? After all, the Lord had just restored senses to a demon-possessed person. The religious leaders could not deny the miracle; but rather than believing that Jesus was the Christ, they attributed the work to Satan. By doing so, they sinned against light. Refusing the light means choosing the darkness. Also, the Pharisees sinned against logic. They had seen with their eyes a blind and dumb man restored to sight and hearing. Rejecting Christ was illogical. The Pharisees sinned against love. Every miracle of Jesus demonstrated his love for humanity. Jesus loved everyone including the self-righteous Pharisees. But they refused to respond to one who genuinely loved them. Their problem was one of the heart. They closed their lives to the possibility of living forever.

Developing an attitude that does not seek God's forgiveness is not God's fault. The sin spoken of in this context does not mean that certain sins cannot be pardoned. It means that some people make themselves unforgivable. John Greenleaf Whittier describes the doom of the unforgiven:

What if thine eye refuse to see,
  Thine ear of Heaven's free welcome fail,
And thou a willing captive be,
  Thyself thine own dark jail?[2]

Another word the Bible uses to speak of the wicked's destiny is *destruction* or *perdition,* two renderings of the Greek word *apoleia.* The New Testament uses the word in general to deal with the fate of the wicked. In John 17:12 Jesus spoke of Judas as "the son of perdition." Also, in 2 Thessalonians 2:3 the word refers to the fate of the Antichrist. Paul spoke of destruction of the wicked, "Who shall be punished with everlasting destruction from the presence of the Lord, and from the glory of his power"

(2 Thes. 1:9). Paul said that destruction is the end of the enemies of the cross (Phil. 3:19-21).

The Bible says that at a definite time the doom of the wicked will be irrevocably fixed. The verses about either *perdition* or *destruction* describe the loss of true life. Jesus warned, "Fear not them which kill the body, but are not able to kill the soul: but rather fear him which is able to destroy both soul and body in hell." *Destroy* does not mean annihilation, but ruin, perdition, and everything that makes existence miserable.

The word *death* is used to describe the destiny of the unsaved. In Revelation 2:10, 11 and 20:6, 14 the fate of the wicked is described with the phrase "second death." The word *death* symbolizes the fallen world (Gen. 3) of separation from and rebellion toward God. Consequently when many Bible writers, especially John, used the word, they did not mean physical death but the consequences of sin and the separation and alienation from God.

The words used to describe hell convince us that it is both real and bad. If the words used to describe its essential character communicate terrible fates, the experience itself must be infinitely worse.

EIGHT
NEITHER FAHRENHEIT
NOR CENTIGRADE

Any discussion of hell would not be complete without some
thought about the degrees of punishment. Many question
whether hell will be the same for all people, wondering if
there will be varying degrees of punishment for the
unrighteous.

Some people believe that every person in hell will suffer
exactly the same way and in the same proportion. Others
believe that eternal punishment will not be the same for all,
that hell's suffering will differ for various reasons.

We know, first of all, that not every person has received
God's eternal life. There is a difference between the life
of the saved and the life of the unsaved. We know also that
the Bible teaches that there are differences in the lives of the
unsaved on earth. Some express their selfishness more
defiantly toward God than others. Some people are simply
worse than others. The Bible appears to teach varying degrees
of punishment for the unsaved. The nature of the differences
is not always clear, but the fact of degrees of punishment
seems to be.

Jesus taught a parable about two servants, one who knew
the master's will, but disobeyed. The other servant didn't
know the master's will, so he didn't do his will either. Yet,

both servants received punishment. "And that servant, which knew his Lord's will, and prepared not himself, neither did according to his will, shall be beaten with many stripes. But he that knew not, and did commit things worthy of stripes, shall be beaten with few stripes" (Luke 12:47, 48). These expressions, "many stripes" and "few stripes," imply a variation in punishment based on how much the servants knew.

Jesus pronounced woes upon the cities of Chorazin, Bethsaida, and Capernaum because they rejected the Lord and his gracious invitations. Jesus said of Chorazin and Bethsaida, "But I say unto you, It shall be more tolerable for Tyre and Sidon at the day of judgment, than for you" (Matt. 11:22). The expression "more tolerable" suggests a difference in condemnation, meaning that Tyre and Sidon would suffer less than Chorazin and Bethsaida.

Jesus also said of Capernaum, "But I say unto you, That it shall be more tolerable for the land of Sodom, in the day of judgment, than for thee" (Matt. 11:24). Capernaum was a pleasant village on the Sea of Galilee, while Sodom had been an extremely wicked place. Sodom had not had the same opportunity, so the condemnation of Capernaum would be greater. The amount of opportunity determines the proportionate severity of judgment.

Paul said, "For we must all appear before the judgment seat of Christ; that every one may receive the things done in his body, according to that he hath done, whether it be good or bad" (2 Cor. 5:10). John A. Broadus said that the doctrine of degrees of punishment "ought to be more prominent in religious instruction. It gives some relief in contemplating the awful fate of those who perish. It might save many from going away into Universalism; and others from dreaming of a second probation in eternity, for which the Scripture gives no warrant."[1]

To understand degrees of punishment in hell we need not wonder whether the temperature is measured in Fahrenheit or centigrade. The Bible shows that there are differences in people on earth, so we can conclude that suffering in hell will not be the same for all.

PEOPLE SEE DIFFERENTLY

Degrees of punishment begin with the diversity of people. Because people are different, they look upon matters differently.

People are also different spiritually. Within each individual is a differing point of view with regard to the Lord. We can't really know why some people can look on God as their precious friend while others view him as their enemy. God makes himself known to every human being. He made it possible for man to have fellowship with him in that he revealed himself to us in ways that suggest his desire to fellowship with us.

There are two primary types of revelation. The first is called *general revelation.* Every person can perceive by the evidences in the natural world, history, and human life, that God exists. Paul wrote: "Because that which may be known of God is manifest in them; for God hath shewed it unto them" (Rom. 1:19). The created universe offers sufficient evidence for anyone to look at the world and know there must be a Master Designer. Francis Bacon said, "God never wrought miracles to convince atheists, because his ordinary works convince it."

The second type of disclosure God has made is called "special revelation," referring to God's mighty acts in the history of Israel and supremely in Jesus Christ. God revealed himself most completely in Jesus Christ, the Word of God. The Bible, the written Word, tells us what God said and did in "salvation-history" and in Jesus.

God made it possible for us to know him. When the Bible speaks of man created in the "image of God" (Gen. 1:26), most scholars agree that the term refers to the spiritual nature of man rather than to a physical form. Man has a measure of affinity with God, and can know and reflect the glory of God.

Even though God has revealed himself, men react differently to what they know. Some open their lives to him, while others refuse. The fault is not God's. The blame is with man's stubbornness. The fact that people see God differently is obvious. If one hears the gospel many times and refuses, hell will contain "many stripes." If one has not heard the gospel frequently and refuses, hell will consist of "few stripes."

Someone might ask, "What about the person who never hears about God's special revelation? Will he go to hell?" The problem of the "heathen" who never hear the gospel of Jesus Christ presents one of the most difficult questions, and many answers are attempted. "Universalism" has a special appeal to many, as it seeks to answer the problem of the heathen by affirming that all will ultimately to go heaven. The very opposite of universalism is the view of some Calvinists. John Calvin contended that God's condemnation could be justly executed upon all men. Some who hold this view contend that God has mercy only upon the elect. For the damned, according to this view, there is nothing that can remove them from the fate of hell.

These two ideas do not seem to fit the Christian gospel. The God revealed in Jesus Christ is just and merciful in his dealings with people. God never seeks anything but a person's highest good. When asking about the heathen or those who never hear the gospel, the Christian finds comfort in Abraham's idea, "Shall not the judge of all the earth do right'" (Gen. 18:25). There does not seem to be a clear answer to the question of the heathen that will please everybody. Nothing must stand in the way of our obeying God's command to go to the entire world with the gospel. Christians must take seriously the words, "He that hath the Son hath life, and he that hath not the Son of God hath not life" (1 John 5:12).

The issue is not really with those who never heard the gospel, but with those who have heard. Jesus cautioned: "Take heed therefore how ye hear: for whosoever hath, to him shall be given; and whosoever hath not, from him shall be taken even that which he seemeth to have" (Luke 8:18).

PEOPLE SIN DIFFERENTLY

Man's morality must be considered in any doctrine of eternal punishment. Just as all do not see God alike, so all do not sin alike. People express their sin differently. In the

parable of the faithful and unfaithful servants in Luke
12:47, 48, both servants sinned, by disobeying the master's
will. Both servants suffered in proportion to their
disobedience. The doctrine of degrees of punishment is
intimately bound with the extent of the sin.

Sin plagues every human being, so the crux of the matter
is how much we express outwardly the inward rebellion
against the Lord. Sin is rebellion against God, and to some
degree, everyone rebels against God. Some rebel harshly and
defiantly. Others resist rather passively. Nonetheless, the
fundamental sin from which all others grow is man's refusal
to acknowledge God's authority in his life.

Sin is man's striving to be the master of his own life and
seeking to find his true existence outside of the Lord's
direction. Sin is an affirmation of self-will against God's will.
Paul said, "There is none righteous, no, not one" (Rom.
3:10). How much one expresses selfishness does not affect the
fact that all selfishness is sin. My two sons are little
leaguers. They consider themselves baseball players just as
much as any big leaguer would. Whether we sin little or
much, we are still sinners.

Both the Bible and human experiences teach us that there
are numerous ways to express the sinful nature. Dallas
Roark compiled from the New Testament a list of 115
different types of sin.[2] In Romans 1:19-31 Paul listed twenty-
one sins of the Gentiles. In Colossians 3:5-12 he mentioned
twelve different kinds of sin.

One category could be the sins of temperament, such as
anger, wrath, malice, and so forth, mentioned throughout
the Bible. Another category could be the sins of the flesh,
attempts to satisfy physical desires.

There are also the social sins. Though some people would
never dare to commit adultery, they hold improper attitudes
toward other people.

Another category includes the sin of omission. "Therefore
to him that knoweth to do good, and doeth it not, to him
it is sin" (Jas. 4:17). Some people live in the world and
become absorbed in world affairs without any thought of
God. They express their rebellion by leaving God out of their
daily lives and future plans, another sin of omission. Some

people sin by being self-righteous. They take pride in their virtues and despise other people. There must be numerous other ways to categorize sin. Every person is a sinner, but we find numerous ways to express it.

If there are varieties of sins, there must be diversities of consequences. Whether adultery is a committed act or a contemplated thought, the matter of guilt is the same. Whether one murders or hates, the guilt prevails. However, the extremely important difference is in the consequences. Reason and logic, as well as the Bible, teach us that people reap different consequences of their sinning. Adultery oftentimes brings unhappiness to children and families. There is also a considerable difference in the consequence between murder and the thought of murder. So there are varieties of sin, though all sin is serious and against God.

PEOPLE SUFFER DIFFERENTLY

The parable of the faithful and unfaithful servants teaches the degrees of punishment. Jesus taught that all of the disobedient suffer. The fact is never in question. The crux is how much. The Bible describes the suffering of the disobedient in terms such as eternal shame, weeping and gnashing of teeth, darkness, destruction, exclusion from God's presence. The biblical expressions, though meta-phorical, give unmistakable glimpses of the reality of suffering, physical and spiritual. No word or expression is graphic enough to describe life outside of Christ. Regarding the symbol of fire, Herschel H. Hobbs said, "If hell is not fire, it is something infinitely worse. No wonder Jesus warned against it so often and so emphatically."[3] The Bible also teaches that the unsaved suffer endlessly. The same word (aionios) used to express the duration of God is used to describe the sufferings of the lost. Out of seventy-one usages of aionios, it applies sixty-four times to the blessed realities of the eternal God. Seven times the word applies to perdition (Matt. 18:8; 24:41; Jude 7; Matt. 25:46; Mark 3:29; 2 Thes. 1:9; and Heb. 6:2). The term forever and ever used frequently in Revelation suggests the endless duration of hell (Rev.

14:11; 19:3; 20:10). Furthermore, the figure of speech implies the endlessness of eternal punishment.

Though Dante was not a biblical expositor, he developed complicated levels of punishment. He subdivided hell or *The Inferno* into nine circles descending to the center of the earth and gradually becoming smaller. The inhabitants suffer according to the gravity of their offense. The inhabitants of the lower parts of *The Inferno* receive the greater punishment. Dante places Lucifer, whom he describes as the fallen angel, at the bottom of hell. Dante placed Judas in the lowest part of the ninth circle of hell. As one proceeds outward the suffering becomes lighter because the offenses were lighter. Reaching such conclusions requires an imaginative mind, but the idea of degrees is based on truth, as we have said.

Extreme caution should be exercised in describing the particulars of the punishment. Jesus never elaborated on the precise nature of the punishment, or what was meant by "beating," "few stripes," or "many stripes."

The degree of sin and the resultant punishment may be seen by looking at two hypothetical people. Both sin against God. One chooses to leave God out of his life completely, breaks the laws of God, robs, murders, and commits adultery. The other man is a respectable community and family man. He is not a thief, adulterer, or a murderer but a good, moral man, well respected in the community. He attends church occasionally, but he does not open his life to Jesus. The Bible teaches that those outside of Christ do not have eternal life. Therefore, both men go to hell. From a human or rational point of view, it would seem that the extremely sinful person should suffer greater than the morally upright person. Both will be separated from God, but it seems that one should be at a greater distance. Speaking imaginatively, the gulf should be wider at the sinful man's section of hell.

Jesus taught that some sins brought greater punishment than others. He said that the scribes "who devour widows' houses, and for a pretense make long prayers . . . shall receive greater condemnation" (Luke 20:45-47). When Jesus spoke of Judas to Pilate, he said, "He that delivered me unto thee hath the greater sin" (John 19:11). Therefore, Jesus regarded some sins as having more guilt than others. Consequently, it would seem that these sins necessitate a greater condemnation.

Imagine some person, well trained in music and able to appreciate good music by outstanding performers and composers. Then, take another example of an amateur's approach to music. This person can appreciate only the beat and rhythm of the popular music. Suppose these two people go together to hear the opera *Madame Butterfly* by Puccini. To the untrained person this masterpiece would probably not be enjoyable, but torture. In the same way, a person unreceptive to God cannot appreciate or comprehend the things of God.

The doctrine of hell is no pleasant subject. But from this study perhaps some insight has been gained about such a serious subject.

This book started with the affirmation that there is a hell, and its essential nature and purpose is described in the Bible. God doesn't want us to go there, but anyone can choose to go if he wants to. The choice is ours.

NOTES

CHAPTER 1
1. Leslie Weatherhead, *The Christian Agnostic* (Nashville: Abingdon Press, 1965), pp. 285-86.
2. Nikolai Berdyaev, *The Destiny of Man*, Trans. Natalie Dudington (London: Geoffrey Bles, Ltd., 1937), p. 338-39.
3. *Science and Health with Key to the Scriptures* (Boston: Published by the trustees under the will of Mary Baker G. Eddy, 1875), p. 588.
4. John Milton, *The Portable Milton*, ed. D. Bush. *Paradise Lost*, Book I, Lines 59-69 (New York: Viking Press, 1949), p. 234.

CHAPTER 2
1. Quoted in Harry Buis, *The Doctrine of Eternal Punishment* (Philadelphia: Presbyterian and Reformed Publishing Company, 1957), p. 104.
2. Emil Brunner, *Eternal Hope* (Philadelphia: Westminster Press, 1954), p. 180.
3. Carl F. H. Henry, *Evangelicals at the Brink of Crisis* (Waco, Texas: Word Books, Publishers, 1967), p. 27.
4. Berdyaev, *op. cit.*, p. 338.
5. Paul Tillich, *Systematic Theology* (Chicago: University of Chicago Press, 1957), II, 284.
6. Charles Haddon Spurgeon, *Spurgeon's Sermons* (Grand Rapids: Zondervan Publishing House, n.d.), IV, 166.
7. John R. W. Stott, *Basic Christianity* (Grand Rapids: Wm. B. Eerdmans Publishing Company, 1958), p. 74.
8. Helmut Thielicke, *The Waiting Father: Sermons on the Parables of Jesus*, Trans. John W. Doberstein (London: James Clarke and Company, Ltd., 1959), p. 48.

CHAPTER 3
1. R. G. Lee, *Bread from Bellevue Oven* (Wheaton, Illinois: Sword of the Lord Publishers, 1951), p. 60.
2. *Ibid.*, p. 52.

3. T. S. Eliot, *The Cocktail Party* (New York: Harcourt Brace Jovanovich, Inc., 1950). Used by permission.
4. Tennessee Williams, *Orpheus Descending with Battle of Angels* (Norfolk, Connecticut: New Directions, 1957).
5. E. Y. Mullins, *The Christian Religion in Its Doctrinal Expression* (Philadelphia: The Judson Press, 1917), p. 496.

CHAPTER 4
1. Jean Paul Sartre, *No Exit and Three Other Plays* (New York: Vintage Books, 1955), p. 44.
2. *Ibid.*, p. 46.
3. George Bernanos, *The Diary of a Country Priest,* Trans. Pamela Morris. (New York: The Macmillan Company, 1937), p. 127.

CHAPTER 5
1. Bernanos, *op. cit.*, p. 16.
2. Quoted in R. Lofton Hudson, *Helping Each Other Be Human* (Waco, Texas: Word Books, Publishers, 1970), pp. 103-104.
3. Quoted in William M. Elliot, Jr., *The Cure for Anxiety* (Richmond: John Knox Press, 1964), p. 37.
4. *Ibid.*, pp. 36-37.
5. "The Testing," *Masterpieces of Religious Verse* (New York: Harper & Row, 1948), p. 187. Reprinted by permission of Mrs. Virgil Markham.
6. William James, *Principles of Psychology* (New York: Henry Holt Company, 1890).
7. Fisher Humphreys, *Thinking About God: An Introduction to Christian Theology* (New Orleans: Insight Press, Inc., 1974), pp. 211-212.

CHAPTER 6
1. Augustus H. Strong, *Systematic Theology* (Philadelphia: Fleming H. Revell Company, 1907), p. 268.
2. John Greenleaf Whittier, as adapted from Strong, *op. cit.*, p. 1042.
3. Quoted in William B. Ward, *After Death, What?* (Richmond: John Knox Press, 1965), p. 66.
4. Berdyaev, *op. cit.*, p. 267.
5. Harold O. J. Brown, *The Protest of a Troubled Protestant* (New Rochelle, New York: Arlington House, 1969), p. 213.

CHAPTER 7
1. A quote in Samuel Smiles, *Selections from Lives of the Engineers,* ed. Thomas Hughes (Cambridge, Massachusetts: Massachusetts Institute of Technology, 1966).
2. John Greenleaf Whittier, "The Answer," *The Complete Poetical works of Whittier* (Boston: Houghton, Mifflin Company, 1848), pp. 441-42.

CHAPTER 8
1. John A. Broadus, "Matthew," *An American Commentary on the New Testament,* ed. Alvah Hovey (Valley Forge: Judson Press, 1886), p. 515.
2. Dallas M. Roark, *The Christian Faith: An Introduction to Christian Thought* (Nashville: Broadman Press, 1969), pp. 217-19.
3. Herschel H. Hobbs, *Fundamentals of Our Faith* (Nashville: Broadman Press, 1960), p. 146.